Praise for The Pre-Paid Legal Story

"Harland Stonecipher is an entrepreneurial pioneer in the Oklahoma tradition. He saw a need and staked his claim. This book is more than a lesson in how-to-make-money; it is also the story of how one man and one company have filled a vital need for many Americans—free enterprise at its freest and most enterprising."

—Frank Keating, governor of Oklahoma

"No longer must one hear, 'You need more justice than you can afford.' Pre-Paid has opened the courthouse doors to all Americans. We can all be thankful for this incredible man and his inspirational and uplifting story."

—Michael C. Turpen, former attorney general of Oklahoma

"We lawyers couldn't provide affordable legal services for the average American until Harland Stonecipher, a non-lawyer, struck a match to light the way. He, more than any other person, is responsible for making the words, 'Equal Justice Under the Law' more than a hollow promise that applies only to the wealthy."

—John Lisle, partner, The Lisle Law Firm, P.A.

"I hail Harland Stonecipher as a pioneer in creating legal access for millions of Americans. His vision continues to sweep away the financial barriers to a legal system that has denied justice to many, if not most, of our people."

—Ronald P. Glantz, past chairman,
American PrePaid Legal Services Institute

"At long last, we learn the inside story of the birth and growth of Pre-Paid Legal Services from its visionary founder who had the foresight and tenacity to revolutionize the delivery of legal services so it would be affordable to the vast majority of Americans. At the same time Harland Stonecipher provides unlimited economic opportunity to any person who joins his multilevel networking program. The story is fascinating and entertaining."

—Sidney S. Friedman, partner,
law firm of Weinstock, Stevan, Harris & Friedman, P.A.

THE PRE–PAID LEGAL STORY

The Story of One Man, His Company,

and Its Mission to Provide

Affordable Legal Protection for Everyone

Harland C. Stonecipher
with James W. Robinson

PRIMA PUBLISHING

3000 Lava Ridge Court • Roseville, California 95661

(800) 632-8676 • www.primalifestyles.com

PRIMA PUBLISHING and colophon are registered trademarks of Prima Communications, Inc.

Library of Congress Cataloging-in-Publication Data on file.

ISBN 0-7615-2221-2

04 05 HH 10 9 8 7 6 5 4 3
Printed in the United States of America

How to Order
Single copies may be ordered from Prima Publishing, 3000 Lava Ridge Court, Roseville, CA 95661; telephone (800) 632-8676. Quantity discounts are also available. On your letterhead, include information concerning the intended use of the books and the number of books you wish to purchase.

Visit us online at http://www.primalifestyles.com

Contents

Harland Stonecipher's story is the greatest best-kept secret, an inspirational, real-life story of overcoming impossible odds to find unbelievable success.

He is a pioneer. He has changed dramatically the landscape of the justice system in this country. He has made the proclamation of "Justice for All" a reality—because before Harland's pioneering dreams, sacrifices, and hard work, one got as much justice as one could pay for.

This is a story of a husband and wife from the Heartland of small-town America who believed they could make a difference, and they did.

They provided a service that every American family should have. For the first time in the United States, they made available the legal help that every small business and home-based business needs and now can afford.

Someday, a monument will be built to honor a man who made this core value of America a reality—that America really is a country with Justice and Liberty for all the People.

    —Fran Tarkenton
      NFL Hall of Fame Quarterback
      Chairman and Founder of GoSmallBiz.com
      Atlanta, Georgia

Chapter 1

IT STARTED
BY ACCIDENT

I started Pre-Paid Legal Services by accident. I mean that quite literally. On an early July morning in 1969, I was driving along a nearly deserted road from Ada, Oklahoma, to Shawnee on my way to an insurance sales meeting. It was Friday and I looked forward to finishing my business and then enjoying a weekend of foxhunting with my wife, Shirley, and all the competitors at the Oklahoma State Hunt, which I helped organize.

It was not meant to be. Just as I approached the crest of a hill, suddenly out of nowhere a car came from the opposite direction and turned left right in front of me! I did my best to avoid a crash, but it was too late. I remember a tremendous blast of breaking glass and bending metal. Then, nothing. When I woke up in Valley

View Hospital back in Ada, the nurse told me that my rescuers had found me in the back seat of my overturned car—just about the only place that wasn't crushed by the time the vehicle hurtled to a stop.

Every time I look at the picture of the accident that appeared in the local paper, I thank God for the fact that I'm still here. My doctors reassured me that while my injuries were severe, my recovery would be complete. After a period of rest and recovery, I would be able to return to work full time to provide for my young family. It was also reassuring to know that my health plan would cover the doctor and hospital bills. My company's auto policy would cover the cost of the totaled car. Considering I had just cheated death, there was a lot to be thankful for.

But then, just as the nightmare of the crash began to fade, a new and totally unexpected nightmare began. I was told that even though the accident was not my fault, I should be ready for a ruinous lawsuit and even a homicide investigation if the woman who was driving the other car died!

Fortunately for her—and for me—she survived. But that didn't stop her from suing. I faced thousands of dollars in legal costs stemming from an accident in which I was blameless—a bill that my wife and I could hardly afford. All because I was in the wrong place at the wrong time.

I told Shirley this would never happen again. Never again would I leave my family in such a vulnerable position. I was astounded that in America you could live your whole life as a hardworking, law-abiding citizen and still wind up as a defendant in a court or the target of legal shakedown that overnight could destroy your finances and even jeopardize your personal freedom.

Before that accident, I thought I had all the bases covered. Being in the insurance business, I knew the value of protecting one's family from the health problems, accidents, and other calamities that could threaten life and property at any time. And I also knew that the most precious benefit of insurance products was the peace of mind they offered. The most contented customer in the world is the one who never has to file a claim. But now I discovered a huge gap in that security and peace of mind, and it just about ruined us. So I told Shirley we were going to get some legal protection as well.

There was just one problem. It didn't exist. Not in Oklahoma. Not anywhere in the United States. The most litigious society in the history of mankind, with ten times the number of lawyers of other advanced societies, did not have for sale an affordable, high-quality legal services plan that would give average citizens access to top-quality lawyers to defend them, advise them, and help them. Justice in America, I

> I was astounded that in America you could live your whole life as a hardworking, law-abiding citizen and still wind up as a defendant in a court or the target of legal shakedown that overnight could destroy your finances and even jeopardize your personal freedom.

learned, had become a high-priced commodity and you get only what you can pay for.

I believe God has a plan for us all and He works His will in what appear to be strange and mysterious ways. I survived a near-fatal accident only to suffer through a legal nightmare. And it was because of that nightmare that I learned about and set out to correct a serious flaw in this, the greatest country on earth—we had a legal system that promised equal justice but failed to deliver on that promise.

So in 1972 I started the precursor company to what is today known as Pre-Paid Legal Services. Our mission is to make the law work for average Americans, just as it's supposed to, and to offer aspiring entrepreneurs a low-cost business opportunity in pursuit of that mission.

What precisely does Pre-Paid Legal do? We develop, underwrite, and market legal service plans nationally and in two Canadian provinces. These plans provide benefits that include unlimited attorney consultation, will preparation, traffic violation defense, defense against automobile-related criminal charges, letter-writing, document preparation and review, and a general trial defense benefit.

The cost of our basic plan is just $14.95 a month and for that, average, middle-class families gain access to the top lawyers in America—the kind of lawyers Bill Gates, Bill Clinton, General Motors, General Electric, and O.J. Simpson can afford!

Today the company serves over 800,000 customers, whom we call members. More than 200,000 independent entrepreneurs sell our products. We call them associates, and many of them earn substantial incomes through commissions on their own sales or by bringing other associates into the business under a network-marketing system.

Both our membership and our independent sales forces are growing phenomenally. In just one recent three-month period, we signed up nearly 135,000 new members and 22,500 new associates.

Each week seems to bring new records. I'll always remember November 30, 1999. On that day, the Monday after a long Thanksgiving holiday weekend, our associate sales force sent a record number of new customer applications pouring in to the headquarters in Ada—over 6,000 in one day.

The record new business was gratifying, but based on the speed at which we're growing it's a record that will soon fall and become rather ordinary before too long. What I'll remember most are the dozens of employees who without complaint stayed into the night—some until 6:00 the next morning—to process that business. That's true dedication, and any employer will tell you that that is harder and harder to find in today's workforce. As soon as all of the employees caught their breath and caught up on their sleep, Shirley had certificates of appreciation made for each person and together we presented them to the best workers any company could ever hope to find.

This kind of enthusiasm for the products and the business opportunity we offer explains why Pre-Paid

Legal is one of the fastest growing companies in America and has been so honored by leading business authorities.

Pre-Paid Legal is a publicly traded company on the prestigious New York Stock Exchange, opening us to full (and welcome) examination by investors, regulators, members, associates, and the media. What they find is:

- a company whose revenues have grown from $60 million in 1996 to $160 million in 1998.
- a company whose sales rose 51 percent over five years, with earnings per share soaring 175 percent over the same period.
- a company that has enjoyed 25 consecutive quarters of revenue and income growth.
- a company with no long-term debt and a cash and investment balance of $42.5 million.
- a company that has been named the 33rd fastest growing company on the New York Stock Exchange.
- a company that ranked number 13 on the *Forbes* magazine list of 200 best small companies in America—the fourth consecutive year we've made it into an exclusive club that applies an extremely difficult set of financial performance standards.
- a company whose network marketing sales force is attracting record numbers of new entries at a time when throughout that industry, domestic growth in recruiting is shrinking or sluggish at best.

And to think all this began "accidentally"!

This book tells the story of the long and winding road we traveled from that car crash back in 1969 to the point today where we are revolutionizing the justice system in America with a simple but compelling legal service product. This is a story not about a new idea but about an old idea that has yet to be put into practice—equal justice under law. And it's a story not so much about what happened yesterday as about what I believe will happen tomorrow.

I call it the thirty-year overnight success story. Our product was not initially accepted—not by a long shot. We have grappled with regulators who didn't trust it, investors who shunned it, lawyers who thought it was beneath their dignity to provide it,

> Our product was not initially accepted— not by a long shot. We have grappled with regulators who didn't trust it, investors who shunned it, lawyers who thought it was beneath their dignity to provide it, and a public that didn't comprehend the need for it.

and a public that didn't comprehend the need for it. These misgivings were not entirely their fault. It took years to perfect our product and our business approach, and I made plenty of mistakes along the way.

As for our embrace of network marketing to distribute our legal services products, I'd like to be able to tell you that I have worshiped at the altar of the multilevel marketing approach from the very start. But I did not. In fact, I had to be dragged kicking and screaming to it.

Just ask John Hail, the fellow who did most of the dragging! To this day, while I am totally committed to our network marketers, we continue to employ a mix of distribution methods, including group sales and alliances with some of the biggest insurance company sales networks in the country. Life is simply too short and the market too big and fragmented to rely on only one distribution method. By the way, I think that's going to be the wave of the future for both traditional companies and network marketing firms—each will borrow the best features of the other to sell products in an increasingly complex marketplace.

I fully subscribe to the observation of Ray Kroc, who was fifty-two and suffering from diabetes and incipient arthritis before he even met two brothers named McDonald and opened his first fifteen-cent hamburger franchise: "Nothing in this world can take the place of persistence. Talent will not; nothing is more common than unsuccessful men with talent. Genius will not; unrewarded genius is almost a proverb. Education will not; the world is full of educated derelicts. Persistence and determination alone are omnipotent."

At Pre-Paid Legal we have persisted for nearly three decades, improving our products, perfecting our business model, and, one family at a time, putting access to justice in the hands of everyday Americans. Through the simple concept of pooling hundreds of thousands of customers and their small monthly fees, we are able to offer unlimited access to the best lawyers in the country, the kind of lawyers that only the rich and famous have been able to afford.

And now I believe our moment has arrived. For nearly three decades we have positioned ourselves to make a lasting positive mark on justice in America. By painstakingly building our customer base, our independent sales force, and our relationship with top law firms, we have reached critical mass in our ability to deliver legal services to a mass market, just as Ray Kroc figured out how to deliver fast food to the world—offer consistent quality, rigorously verified; charge an affordable price; provide familiarity and comfort; and give people not just a product but an opportunity along with it. There is no doubt in my mind that we are now poised for explosive growth. The dawn of our thirty-year overnight success has finally arrived.

And not a moment too soon. The justice system in America is broken and it needs fixing. The legal profession in America is ridiculed and reviled—and it needs to be revitalized. Entrepreneurship in America has become too expensive—and it needs to be put back in the hands of ordinary people once again.

Hardly a day goes by when we don't hear about an alleged miscarriage of justice: rogue police officers who abuse suspects; law enforcement agencies who use racial profiling to determine who to pull over on the highway; and juries that are swayed by emotion rather than facts, manipulated by hired-gun psychologists to free the guilty or convict the innocent. Hardly a day goes by when we don't hear about a ridiculous lawsuit instigated by greedy attorneys, a settlement in which most or all of the money goes to the lawyers while their class-action clients go empty-handed, or litigation that shuts down a small business or a community activity. And hardly a day goes by when we don't hear about some new tax, regulation, or other costly burden piled onto the backs of America's struggling entrepreneurs, making the already long odds for small business success even longer.

Because we've worked hard to perfect our products, our relationships with the legal profession, and our business opportunity, Pre-Paid Legal is ideally positioned today for tremendous growth—not because we're so smart but because the conditions facing justice, lawyers, and entrepreneurs cry out for innovative solutions and bold reform.

People who know me say I am a man with a mission. I guess they're right. Get me started on the shortcomings of justice in this country and how our concept addresses them, and there's no stopping me. Our friends have asked Shirley, who travels with me all over the United States to spread the message, if she ever gets tired of listening to me on my soapbox. She just smiles and says no, never. That's because she believes in the mission as much as I do, and without her counsel, support, and love, there would be no such thing as Pre-Paid Legal Services.

And I am often asked, Why Ada, Oklahoma? Having reached a respectable degree of success, why not move to one of the country's great business centers where the stage is larger and the platform for success so much stronger?

It's very simple. I grew up in the beautiful rolling hills of central Oklahoma, and I'm never going to leave. Thankfully, in this era of high-speed transportation and instantaneous electronic communication, you can run a successful business from almost anywhere. But what you can't find in very many places is a close-knit community where loyal, hardworking employees pour their hearts into a company. At Pre-Paid Legal, we have dozens of employees among the four hundred in our headquarters who have been with us since the beginning. Ask virtually any CEO in America what his or her number-one long-term headache is, and the answer will be—finding capable, dedicated, hardworking employees. We don't have that headache in Ada, Oklahoma.

So I'm proud to have the opportunity to put something back into the community that gave this son of dirt-poor sharecroppers an opportunity to pursue the American dream. And it's gratifying to help put God's country on the map—at least, that's what many of our big city guests call it when they visit Ada for the first time!

> We will do everything in our power for the rest of our lives to help America finally keep its most solemn promise: the promise of Equal Justice Under Law.

As for Shirley and me, we think we're the luckiest people in the world to have been able to stand in the

New York Stock Exchange and ring the opening bell on the day our company started trading there—and then beat a path back to Oklahoma, to our farm, our family, our company, and our sixty hounds. From here, we will do everything in our power for the rest of our lives to help America finally keep its most solemn promise: the promise of Equal Justice Under Law.

Chapter 2

THE MYTH OF EQUAL JUSTICE

Consider two places, one famous, one infamous. The west wall of the most beautiful building in Washington, D.C., the United States Supreme Court—and the bathroom of a Brooklyn police station in New York City.

On the west wall of the Supreme Court, engraved in marble, is a simple but eloquent phrase: Equal Justice Under Law. It's the foundation on which the greatest country on earth is based. A simple phrase, a powerful concept. It tells us that no matter what your background, your wealth, your age, sex, race, religion, or national origin, you are promised equal justice under law. It's a right that will ultimately be defended by the one institution in the greatest democracy in history, which puts the rights

13

of the lone individual above the collective will or prejudices of the many—the United States Supreme Court.

We must unfortunately return to the toilet in that Brooklyn precinct house. That's where such unspeakable acts were committed against a Haitian immigrant named Abner Louima that television newscasters fumbled for polite, dinner-table ways to describe them.

O n the west wall of the Supreme Court, engraved in marble, is a simple but eloquent phrase: Equal Justice Under Law. There's just one problem with the concept. It's not true. It just isn't true.

What happened is that on a hot August night in 1997, Louima was arrested following a disturbance outside a New York City nightclub. During the course of questioning at the precinct house, he was beaten and then shoved into the bathroom by NYPD officer Justin Volpe and then sodomized with the broken-off handle of a broomstick. The stick was then waved under his nose as Volpe warned him that if he ever told anyone what had happened, he would be killed.

Yet Abner Louima's internal injuries were so severe that he had to be hospitalized. Covering up what had happened would be tough—even with police officers' time-honored "code of silence." Questions were asked. People started talking—including Abner.

One of the people he talked to was a nurse who cared for him as he recovered in the hospital from surgery to repair his terrible injuries. As recounted in news reports, she listened incredulously and said, "You really ought to get a lawyer." The officer who did this to him should not get away with it. Who would be next?

Two years later, Officer Volpe pleaded guilty to his crime and was sentenced to a long prison term. He expressed great remorse for the dishonor he had brought to his own family but offered only a few halting words of regret to his victim. Several other officers were implicated in a cover-up that eventually blew wide open. *Newsweek* magazine concluded that Abner Louima "might never have told his story if a hospital nurse hadn't told him to get a lawyer."

Think about that. The first time that young immigrant got any legal advice during his whole ordeal was after he landed in the hospital. And when he did, he got it from a nurse. He had no idea what his rights were. No idea about how to access the justice system. No idea how to shield himself upon arrest with a polite but firm assertion of his rights.

Equal justice under law? How do we in the greatest nation on earth reconcile the promise engraved on that beautiful building in Washington, D.C., with the reality of that broomstick attack in the bathroom of that Brooklyn precinct house?

You know as well as I do that we cannot and should not.

Maybe you are thinking that what happened to Abner Louima was a rare, isolated incident—a terrible case of a rogue cop who lost all control but who, after all, was eventually caught and punished. It is surely an extreme example, but don't think that others like it and many other less-extreme miscarriages of justice don't occur every day across our country.

Ada, Oklahoma, population 18,000, is about as far away as you can get from the skyscrapers and subways of New York City. It's a peaceful, family-oriented community with decent people—the pure definition of Middle America.

My son Brent told me recently about a young man he went to high school with who ended up on the wrong side of the law. Brent hadn't seen him in quite a while and was shocked by how he'd changed—he was now a physically and emotionally broken young man who had obviously been through a terrible ordeal. Apparently, he and a friend had been picked up for a drug-related arrest and thrown into a large holding cell with other prisoners. While they were behind bars, someone—perhaps a sadistic guard, we can only guess—spread the word that the two young men were actually police informants. The other inmates were enraged and savagely beat them. The young men survived but will never really be the same.

Now, I'm totally opposed to illegal drug use. Those who are caught should be punished, just like other truly guilty criminals. We must never forget that catching and punishing the lawbreakers to protect the law-abiding citizens in our society is part of equal justice as well!

But what was done to those young men was criminal, too. It shouldn't happen to anyone in this country. I don't care if they were lawbreakers, they have rights. And I wondered, while hearing this story, if the outcome might have been different if they had had the knowledge and the wherewithal to exercise those rights upon their arrest.

What those young men didn't have was connections. They didn't have money. They weren't equipped with the knowledge or the tools to assert themselves. Therefore, they didn't get justice.

A System of Injustice

New York City or Ada, Oklahoma. The sad results spring from the same cause. We don't have a system of justice in America but a system of injustice. Most of the people in it—the judges, the lawyers, the cops, and the prosecutors—are good people. It's the system that's broken and desperately needs to be fixed.

For most Americans, the impact of our failure to do so will not be nearly as severe as it was for Abner Louima in New York City or for those young men in Ada. But for that individual, law-abiding American who suddenly for some reason finds himself caught up in the grinding wheels of the system and finds that the promise of justice is not kept, it is the most important thing in the world at the time.

There's no more disturbing example of how this can happen than the inexcusable practice of racial profiling.

As a white American, it's hard for me to understand the depth of anger and indignity that is felt by an African American or a member of another minority group when, in a sea of traffic on the streets, they are the ones pulled over for routine checks. Or when they are eyed suspiciously and questioned for driving or even walking through an upscale neighborhood. Or maybe their sports car is just a little too fancy for the likes of a patrolman who has come to believe that the only way the driver could afford such a car is if he were engaged in illegal activity.

The easy answer for those who don't have to worry about being stereotyped is to say, "Well, if you've done nothing wrong, you've got nothing to worry about." But try to put yourself in the shoes of this man: He's an African American who worked his way up from an impoverished background. He had scrapes with the law as a youth but ultimately rejected gangs and drugs and put himself through college and law school. He then dedicated his life to working as a prosecutor to locking up criminals who were terrorizing his and other communities—only to find that the system routinely treated him like one of those criminals!

I'm talking about O.J. Simpson prosecutor Christopher Darden, a black man who was totally convinced of Mr. Simpson's guilt and who worked day and night to debunk the defense theory that Mr. Simpson was an innocent victim of a racial frame-up. Nonetheless, Mr. Darden has described with weary resignation the many times he was singled out and pulled over by the police for driving through the "wrong" neighborhood (a rich one) in the "wrong" kind of car (a Porsche) in the "wrong" kind of clothes (a three-piece designer business suit).

Then there's the case of U.S. Army Sergeant First Class Rossano V. Gerald—a highly decorated veteran of Desert Storm who is black and of Panamanian descent—and his young son Gregory. On a hot August day in 1998, they crossed the Oklahoma border and within thirty minutes they were stopped "randomly" by the Highway Patrol not once but twice!

David Harris, a University of Toledo College of Law professor who has documented many real-life cases of racial profiling, describes what happened: "During the second stop, which lasted two-and-a-half hours, the troopers terrorized SFC Gerald's twelve-year-old son with a police dog, placed both father and son in a closed car with the air conditioning turned off and fans blowing hot air, and warned that the dog would attack if they attempted to escape.

"How did it come to be that . . . SFC Gerald found himself standing on the side of a dusty road next to a barking police dog, listening to his son weep while officers rummaged through his belongings simply because he was black? Rossano and Gregory Gerald were victims of discriminatory racial profiling by police."

This career soldier and decorated war hero has filed a lawsuit over the incident, explaining, "I'm an authority figure myself. I don't want my son thinking for one minute that this kind of behavior by anyone in uniform is acceptable."

Acceptable behavior? Of course not. But a common occurrence? Unfortunately, the evidence is mounting that it is. In fact, minority communities victimized by it have bitterly coined an expression, playing on the words "driving while intoxicated": DWB, which means "driving while black (or brown)."

In the state of Illinois, for example, a special drug interdiction effort called Operation Valkyrie relied on the traffic code to stop motorists who were then searched for drugs if officers could establish just cause. Who was stopped is revealing and disturbing: Hispanics, who account for less than 8 percent of the Illinois population and 3 percent of the state's vehicle trips, comprised 30 percent of vehicle stops and 27 percent of the searches made in Operation Valkyrie.

> In America today, you're going to get just as much justice as you can pay for. That's because we've transformed it from a right into a commodity.

Our criminal justice system is made up of human beings whose conduct is governed by human frailties, fears, and upbringing. I have tremendous respect for the men and women of law enforcement. I can't imagine any group of people who have tougher jobs. As Los Angeles Police Chief Bernard Parks, himself an African American, has said: "Police officers are the only group of Americans who, when they hear gunfire, they run *towards* it."

There can be no excuse for our nation's failure to live up to the promise of equal justice under law—and yet we are failing in many ways every day. Law enforcement's role in this failure accounts for but a small fraction of the problem.

Who Loses When Justice Becomes a Commodity?

It's a simple equation. In America today, you're going to get just as much justice as you can pay for. That's because we've transformed it from a right into a commodity.

Who loses? Not the very rich. The top 10 percent of Americans and the large corporations can afford the services of the best lawyers. They put lawyers on retainer or hire them full time and access their services on a regular basis. And if you're poor, although you certainly face many hurdles in life, you have access to the public defender system, can take advantage of government-funded legal services, and are often first in line for conscience-driven pro bono work by for-profit law firms.

But if you are part of Middle America—and that's where most of us are—you're left out and left behind.

Most middle-class Americans don't know any lawyers. Maybe you don't, either. Lawyers intimidate you.

You're concerned about what legal advice will cost. And you're figuring that as a law-abiding citizen without a big fortune or complicated financial dealings, you should be able to make it through life without confronting the need to defend yourself, your good name, your family, your freedom, your right to drive, or your financial security. Curling up with a good John Grisham novel is about as close to the justice system as you ever want to get!

Now, I don't have a problem with the fact that some people can't afford to drive a Lincoln or a Cadillac and have to drive a Ford or a Chevy instead. Cars are a commodity, pure and simple. But I have a real problem with the fact that justice has become a commodity. If you can't pay, you don't play. As Derek Bok, former president of Harvard University, has written:

"There is far too much law in America for those who can afford it and far too little for those who cannot. No one can be satisfied with this state of affairs. The cost of hiring a lawyer and the mysteries of the legal process discourage most people of modest means from trying to enforce their rights.

"The blunt, inexcusable fact is that this nation, which prides itself on efficiency and justice, has developed a legal system that is the most expensive in the world, yet cannot manage to protect the rights of most of its citizens."

He's exactly right. There are plenty of laws and more than enough lawyers, yet for reasons of cost, lack of information, and systemic bias, 80 percent of Americans—100 million middle-class families—don't readily access them. They don't know how to and don't think they can.

Lawyers—Who Needs Them?

How likely is it that the typical, law-abiding, middle-class American will end up in court? If recent statistics are any guide, you are three times more likely to wind up in court than in a hospital. There are more than 33 million hospitalizations in our country each year—but more than 100 million court filings! For the statistically minded, that's 273,972 filings a day; 11,415 an hour; 190 each minute; and just over 3 every second. Do you think it can't happen to you? I used to—until that car accident! That's when I found out that a legal action could wipe out all I had worked for and struggled to achieve—and I wasn't even the one at fault!

According to the American Bar Association (ABA), more than half of all households are facing a legal situation right now. And the National Resources Center for Consumers of Legal Services has found that even law-abiding Americans will encounter a potential legal situation an average of four to six times a year. The problem is, they don't know where to turn or don't believe they can afford legal counsel when they do encounter these situations. So, many people simply ignore the problem or try to handle it themselves.

And have a fool for a client, as the lawyers' old saying goes!

When it comes to the need for legal service, it's not a question of if but a question of when.

That's especially true when it comes to a condition anyone has yet to find a cure for—death!

Perhaps you're one of the millions who see no need to prepare a will. I've had folks tell me, "I came into this life with no worldly possessions and I'll leave just about the same way. What I do have left will automatically go to my closest next of kin, so why spend up to $1,000 or more for a will? There'll be nothing to fight over, anyway!"

But how do you know? Suppose your death is judged a wrongful one—a plane crash, for example. No doubt, there will be a class-action lawsuit and a settlement that could pump hundreds of thousands of dollars, if not millions, into your estate. Nothing to fight over?

What about your final illness? Do you want extraordinary life-saving measures to be taken no matter what your condition, or is there a point when you want to pass on with dignity? And whom do you want or trust to make such a fateful decision? How about special stipulations for beloved pets, cherished family heir-

> If recent statistics are any guide, you are three times more likely to wind up in court than in a hospital. There are more than 33 million hospitalizations in our country each year—but more than 100 million court filings!

looms, relatives you were especially fond of or who have special needs, or charitable causes you want to be remembered for?

What if tragedy was to befall you and your spouse at the same time? Do you know what the law stipulates will happen to your minor children? Wouldn't you like to make that decision?

A lot of "what if" questions, you are thinking, and macabre ones at that. Sure, it's easier and more comfortable to just keep whistling past the graveyard. But when you buy health insurance, you generally don't know what illness or treatment you're buying it for (and if you did, good luck finding someone to sell it to you!). You deal with "what if" questions when it comes to your family's health, home, and car insurance because you want peace of mind and you figure that sooner or later the odds of illness or accident will tilt against you.

The Three Pillars of Equal Justice

I'm convinced that if individuals simply learned how to exercise their rights, if they could access the justice system in the same way the rich and powerful can, many of the abuses we hear about today would end and we would see confidence restored in our system.

The justice system—not just the laws and the courts but the legal profession as well—should be accessible and be put to work for every American in three critical ways. Only then can we say that the promise of equal justice is being kept.

First, the justice system must stand as the last line of defense for the individual in a free society. No matter what you may have done—or not done—you should have the right to due process in a court of law with a committed and capable attorney handling your defense. The system ought to treat your case with the same care and seriousness as that of any powerful executive or famous celebrity. And it is the state's burden to prove your guilt, not your burden to prove your innocence.

Second, the justice system should be used as a preventative tool to keep you from landing in legal situations and disputes in the first place. By consulting capable attorneys before you sign contracts, make agreements, or take action against others, such as employees, tenants, or neighbors, you can prevent costly and time-consuming problems down the road.

Third, the justice system should be a resource that gives you as much clout and gains you as much attention for your grievances as it does for the rich and well connected.

When the CEO of a big corporation sends a letter on his stationery to a supplier who didn't deliver as promised, a customer who didn't pay, or a government agency that's dragging its feet, you can bet that letter moves to the top of the pile. But when John Smith of Anytown, U.S.A., sends such a letter to a big corporation or government bureaucrat on plain paper in a handwritten envelope with a 33-cent stamp stuck on it a little crooked, how much fast attention do you think he will get?

Now picture the same complaint from the same John Smith, but this one presented on the letterhead of one of the top law firms in the country. It may not move ahead of the powerful CEO's, but it won't be too far behind!

Most Americans have no idea of the results they can get from the justice system if they put it to work on their behalf in these three ways:

o as a line of defense when they stand accused or are sued
o as a preventative tool to forestall problems and actions against them
o as a resource to gain a fair hearing for their own grievances

With proper guidance from experienced, top-quality law firms, average Americans could creatively employ each of these three pillars of equal justice and learn some important truths about today's complicated legal environment. For example, did you know?

o You should never simply plead guilty to a moving traffic violation and send in the money.
o How quickly and under how many different circumstances the good neighbor next door can turn into a legal adversary.

○ How fast teams of corporate lawyers will come after you if you've done something wrong or how readily they will ignore your complaints if they believe there will be no consequences.

○ How quickly those same corporations will settle with you if they sense big-time trouble should you have a top law firm on your side.

○ You should never waive your rights and talk to the police if taken into custody, no matter how soothing their words or reassuring their claims that "we can get this resolved quickly."

Most Americans do not understand their most important rights or the many ways they can find themselves on the receiving end of a legal action. In December 1999, we learned that the Supreme Court would hear and decide a case on whether the famous Miranda decision is grounded in the Constitution—in other words, whether you do indeed have a constitutional right to be advised that "you have the right to remain silent. If you give up the right to remain silent, anything you say can and will be used against you in a court of law." When this important news was announced, the *New York Times* was among those media outlets whose reports told the disturbing truth: that the impact of the Court's impending decision could be limited no matter how it rules, because "most people waive their Miranda rights anyway."

And as Americans prepared to celebrate the arrival of a new century and new millennium at the end of 1999, they were warned quite properly that if they hosted a New Year's Eve party in their home and a guest drank over the legal limit and caused an accident while driving home, the hosts could be subject to a huge lawsuit that might cost them their house or, under some circumstances, expose them to charges of criminal negligence!

When people ask me to give them one good reason why they might need legal protection, I drive my point home by telling them I can't give them one, but I can give them 101! It's a list to which readers, reflecting on the circumstances of their own lives, could surely add many others:

101 Reasons Why You Need Legal Protection

1. Your car insurance is canceled when your teenage son is involved in an accident.
2. A neighbor's child is injured playing in your yard.
3. Your dog bites an elderly passerby.
4. The auto repair shop threatens small claims court for money you don't owe.
5. The IRS selects you for an audit.
6. A tenant falls down stairs and sues you for negligence.
7. Your child throws a baseball through a neighbor's car window.
8. A merchant refuses to honor a guarantee.
9. You have an accident driving your friend's boat.

10. Your deceased spouse didn't have an up-to-date will.

11. A minor is caught breaking into your home.

12. Your driver's license is suspended.

13. Your landlord raises your rent in violation of a verbal agreement.

14. Your teenager is accused of shoplifting.

15. You decide to change your name.

16. You are cited with DWI/DUI charges while taking medication.

17. Creditors threaten to take action against you for your ex-spouse's debts.

18. A neighbor reports you for child abuse.

19. You decide to adopt.

20. A friend is injured on your property and sues you.

21. Family members challenge your parents' will.

22. You are buying a new home.

23. A stranger calls and demands money or damaging information will be released.

24. Your car is damaged by a hit-and-run driver.

25. You accidentally back over a neighbor's garbage can that was not in its proper place.

26. A hairdresser damages your hair with harsh chemicals.

27. Your child wrecks the car, and a friend is injured.

28. You are subpoenaed.

29. You are called to jury duty.

30. Your long drive off the tee injures another player.

31. You need a lease agreement reviewed.
32. Your son is injured in a football game.
33. A neighbor trips over a rake in your yard and breaks a leg.
34. A jeweler sells you faulty merchandise.
35. A car dealership gains illegal access to your credit history.
36. You are hit by a bottle at a baseball game.
37. Your parents die and leave you executor of their estate.
38. Your dog is poisoned.
39. You are injured when you slip on a wet floor in a public building.
40. Your dogs trample a neighbor's garden.
41. Your neighbor's dog barks for hours every night.
42. Your teenager gets a speeding ticket.
43. Your landlord enters your apartment without permission.
44. You need an attorney's advice on any matter.
45. A neighbor's dog attacks and injures your pet.
46. Your landlord refuses to refund your cleaning deposit.
47. You lose an expensive watch in a hotel and the manager claims no liability.
48. Your boat is damaged while in storage.
49. A speeding car nicks your bumper while you are parked in the street.
50. You need a letter written on your behalf by an attorney.

51. You need a phone call on your behalf by an attorney.
52. Your spouse claims a right to your earnings.
53. A record club sends you merchandise after you canceled your membership.
54. You are refused service at a restaurant.
55. A property manager refuses to rent to you.
56. You are denied credit for no apparent reason.
57. You are fired without just cause.
58. You receive a ticket for speeding.
59. You don't have a will.
60. You don't understand the difference between a trust and a will.
61. You made a sizable gift to charity.
62. Angry words result in a slander suit.
63. You need a patent for an invention.
64. You need a copyright for your manuscript.
65. You are wrongly accused of committing a crime.
66. Your right to privacy has been invaded.
67. Your car is vandalized in a parking lot.
68. A postal carrier slips on your unshoveled walk and breaks his leg.
69. Your daughter is dating someone you don't approve of, and you want to know how much authority you have under the law.
70. You are stopped for speeding, and a friend riding in your car is in possession of marijuana.
71. Your teenager backs over a friend's mailbox.

72. A store will not sell you an article because it has the wrong price tag attached.

73. You are cheated by an e-commerce Web site.

74. A salesman charges more than a given estimate.

75. A creditor tries to put you in jail for owing money.

76. A year-old accident results in a personal injury.

77. Your car is repossessed unjustly.

78. You are scheduled to appear in small claims court.

79. Your new house has bad plumbing and a leaky roof.

80. Your neighbors ruin the neighborhood with loud parties and failing to mow their lawn.

81. You are about to join a health club.

82. You are selling your home.

83. You have a minor fender bender while driving a friend's car.

84. You have liability questions in launching a new business.

85. Your neighbor's dog bites your child.

86. You have a property line dispute over a newly installed fence.

87. You're an eyewitness to a robbery and are asked to testify in trial.

88. You need a premarital agreement.

89. You are buying or selling a car.

90. You have an altercation in a nightclub and threatening remarks are made.

91. Your bank sends a foreclosure notice after one house payment is late.
92. A retail store won't accept the return of defective merchandise.
93. A pool repairman won't stand behind his work.
94. A trespasser is caught poaching on your land.
95. You are leasing land.
96. Contractors leave a home improvement project unfinished.
97. A bank unjustly turns you in to a credit bureau.
98. You need advice concerning a divorce.
99. You need advice concerning grounds for adultery.
100. Your neighbor's tree limbs overhang your yard and create a hazard.
101. Your spouse uses force against you.

All it takes is one, not 101—one unforeseen legal action that can wreck your family's finances or ruin its good name. Or worse, a miscarriage of justice that in extreme cases could jeopardize your health, your freedom, or even your life. Think again about the issue of racial profiling. The words of a young African-American mother of a teenage son are haunting. When her son first started to drive, she told him:

"The police are supposed to be there to protect you, but you being black and being male, you've got two strikes against you. Keep your hands on the steering wheel, and do not run, because they will shoot you in the back. Let them do whatever they want to do. I know it's humiliating, but let them do whatever they want to do to make sure you get out of that situation alive. Deal with your emotions later. Your emotions are going to come second—or last."

The justice system in America is broken and needs to be fixed. But how and by whom? The first and most natural place to look would seem to be those in charge of it—the lawyers. Guess again.

Chapter 3

TOO MANY LAWSUITS—NOT ENOUGH JUSTICE

Let every American, every lover of liberty, every well-wisher to his posterity, swear by the blood of the Revolution, never to violate in the least particular the laws of the country; and never to tolerate their violation by others. Let reverence for the laws be breathed by every American mother, to the lisping babe that prattles in her lap—let it be taught in schools, in seminaries, and in colleges; let it be written in primers, spelling books, and in almanacs; let it be preached from the pulpit, proclaimed in legislative halls, and enforced in the courts of justice.

In short, let it become the *political religion* of the nation.

—ABRAHAM LINCOLN,
in a speech to the Young Men's Lyceum,
Springfield, Illinois, 1837,
reacting to an outbreak of lawlessness
and mob rule throughout the United States

Our greatest president understood more than 160 years ago what we as a nation still fail to understand—that both lawbreaking and miscarriages of justice carry far greater consequences than those suffered by the innocent victim or the falsely accused. There is a corrosive effect that undermines the confidence and credibility of civil society itself. People have to believe in the system. They have to trust it to be fair. When people stop believing that the system is fair or that it can adequately protect them from harm, their cynicism encourages further lawbreaking by criminals, corner-cutting by law enforcement, plea-bargaining by lawyers and prosecutors, and greater cynicism among average Americans.

Who can deny that that is exactly what is happening today? The justice system has become a game. On the criminal side, the public's frustration grows as it watches legal dissembling turn plain truth on its ear. In the racially charged trials of the Los Angeles police officers who beat Rodney King, the rioters who beat Reginald Denny in revenge for the officers' acquittal, and, of course, O.J. Simpson, Americans (and, most likely, jurors) chose sides based not on facts and evidence but on sympathies and prejudices. The justice system was something to game and manipulate—not to use to find the truth. However one personally feels about the guilt or innocence of each of those defendants, there is no doubt that the justice system itself was on trial and it was found guilty on all counts.

Another flaw was brought home by the interminable Simpson trial. It was the defendant's ability to access millions and millions of dollars' worth of top legal talent, which determined the trial's pace and in the eyes of many altered its outcome. If the average middle-class American had been on trial, it may have lasted a week. If the defendant were a poor unknown from the inner city instead of a sports hero celebrity living in a gated estate, the trial would have been even shorter. The system loves the rich and can't afford to love anyone else.

What Americans Think About Justice

Americans appear wearily resigned to this reality. In early 1999, the American Bar Association released a comprehensive national survey that found broad support for the basic principles of American justice, especially when compared to other countries, but deep doubts as to whether those principles were being met. The report revealed that:

○ Only 30 percent expressed a great deal of confidence in the U.S. justice system overall.
○ A substantial number of people believed that the justice system treats different groups of people unequally. Only about half agreed that men and women are treated equally; even fewer believed

that among racial or ethnic groups or between wealthy and poor people, the treatment is equal.

○ An overwhelming 90 percent agreed that "wealthy people or companies often wear down their opponents by dragging out legal proceedings."

○ Respondents also believed that "court costs are too high, that court matters take too long to resolve; that certain groups are not treated fairly in court; that judges and lawyers should perform more community service."

○ Confidence is further undercut by a belief that the system is failing to swiftly and adequately punish the truly guilty. "Anywhere from one-half to three-quarters of respondents feel that convicted criminals have too many opportunities to appeal (72 percent), that they are set free on too many technicalities (68 percent), and that they are not given severe enough punishment (52 percent)."

○ And many Americans lack a deep or even basic knowledge about their rights or the workings of American justice. Using a series of questions as a measuring stick, the ABA found that only 26 percent could be considered highly knowledgeable about the justice system. Just 17 percent could name the chief justice of the United States. And even though the most basic tenet of our system is that one is "innocent until proven guilty," the ABA survey discovered that "astonishingly, a third of the respondents believe that the defendant must prove innocence rather than that the prosecutor must prove guilt."

Frivolous Lawsuits— What Will They Think of Next?

If the criminal justice system has become a game, then civil justice in America has become a joke. It's a legal lottery in which a handful of class-action trial lawyers enrich themselves through specious claims and frivolous lawsuits, while real victims deserving real redress go unserved and unrepresented.

For the lucky few who win the lottery, the results can be pretty good:

> If the criminal justice system has become a game, then civil justice in America has become a joke.

- o A New Mexico woman buys a cup of coffee from a McDonald's drive-thru, spills the hot coffee in her lap, and sues the fast food giant. A jury awards her more than $2 million.
- o A Port Isabel, Texas, man injures his knee when a small dog runs in front of his bicycle. He sues and is awarded $1.8 million.
- o A drunken San Antonio man wanders into a public stairwell to urinate, falls down, and injures his back. He sues and wins $8,000 in damages.

41

Then there are those who give it the old college try, hoping they'll find a gullible jury, a sympathetic judge, or a defendant who figures it's cheaper to pay them to just go away rather than fight them through the courts.

Each year, San Antonians Against Lawsuit Abuse, a group of legal reform activists, compiles what it believes are the wackiest lawsuits of the year. With thanks and acknowledgment to the group, here is its list for 1999:

1. Man Kan't Spel, Sues Instead

The *Sacramento Bee* reports that a twenty-three-year-old man is seeking $25,000 in damages from a tattoo parlor for misspelling the word *villain* on his right forearm. The problem is, the incorrect spelling, *villian,* came from the man himself, who was unsure as to the spelling of the word upon entering the parlor. After much debate, he settled on the incorrect spelling. In fact, he didn't even notice the error until years later, when a friend made fun of him.

Claiming that the tattoo cost $1,900 to remove and left a scar on his forearm, the man is now asking for $25,000 for his own mistake.

2. Woman Sues After Being Left in Doghouse

A deceased millionaire has left his longtime female companion in the financial doghouse in favor of another companion, his pet dog.

Reuters reports that a man, who passed away in 1996, left $350,000 in his will to his fifteen-year-old cocker spaniel, Samantha. He also left Samantha his Beverly Hills mansion, valued at $5 million. Meanwhile, his thirty-two-year-old longtime companion, was left an annual stipend of $60,000 and is allowed to live in the mansion, provided she cares for Samantha. The will also stipulates that when Samantha dies, she loses her stipend and the house is to be sold. The proceeds of the sale are to be donated to animal charities.

The woman is suing for half of the estate.

3. Class Doesn't Click for Students

According to the *San Antonio Express-News,* a dozen students who took a Microsoft computer certification course at the Houston branch of Southern Methodist University are suing the school, contending they were misled that the course would be easy.

The twelve enrolled in June 1997, and all failed the certification tests that would have made them eligible for jobs overseeing Microsoft computer systems. "They were told all they had to know how to do was point a mouse and click," the group's attorney said.

4. Fugitive Financier Sued for Ruining the Neighborhood

Three neighbors of a fugitive money manager filed suit against him in the state court in Connecticut, alleging that his notoriety had significantly decreased the value of their multi-million-dollar homes and that he should make up their losses.

The man vanished in May when state and federal authorities closed in on him, in search of hundreds of millions of dollars belonging to insurance companies he controlled and whose investments he handled.

The Associated Press quoted plaintiffs as claiming that scores of law enforcement officials and journalists have ruined the tranquillity of their neighborhood, and it is now "associated with criminal activity."

According to the suit, a real estate broker hired by the plaintiffs estimated that the value of their houses had decreased by about 20 percent—and the houses are now worth $2.4 million and $3.2 million each.

5. The Drunk of the Irish

In Orlando, a lawsuit was filed against a rental car company by the estate of a woman who was killed in a car crash by a drunk driver. The woman was riding in a rental car driven by her boyfriend, an Irish tourist, who was legally drunk. He was eventually charged with manslaughter and driving under the influence.

The suit alleges that the rental car company should be liable for the woman's death because the company "either knew or should have known about the unique cultural and ethnic customs in Ireland which involve the regular consumption of alcohol at pubs as a major component to Irish social life."

6. Mother Files Suit to Make Son a Valedictorian

The mother of a high school student who was allowed to skip his senior year of classes and take college classes instead has filed a lawsuit against the school district because it didn't make him valedictorian. The plaintiff seeks to force the school district to calculate the grade point average of her son, counting his As at Pennsyvania State University as comparable to A pluses in high school, and to name him valedictorian if the calculation makes him come out the highest-ranking member of his graduating class.

According to the lawsuit, the family had agreed to forfeit his chance at being valedictorian at his high school if he were allowed to take the college classes.

The *Philadelphia Inquirer* reported that although Judge Michael Kane refused to order a hearing on the lawsuit, the family appealed that ruling to Commonwealth Court and sought to have the decision overturned before the school's graduation ceremony.

The student has accepted an academic scholarship to Franklin and Marshall College.

7. Woman Sues Airline, Says She Was Trampled in Line

A Kentucky woman claims she was trampled by passengers at a Houston airport two years ago while waiting in line for a ticket. She is now suing the airline for unspecified damages.

The woman blames the airline for creating the "mad rush" of humanity that knocked her to the ground. It wasn't just her pride that was stepped on. The suit claims she suffered a cartilage tear in her knee requiring two surgeries.

According to the suit, an airline employee announced that the flight had been canceled and that seats on the next available flight could be had on a first-come, first-served basis. The woman's attorney claims that the airline should not have announced the alternative plan over the public address system.

8. Lather, Rinse, Litigate

The *Fort Lauderdale Sun-Sentinel* reports that, citing liability concerns, officials at the Town Center Club of Bonaventure and Century Village in Pennbroke Pines, Florida, have banned soap from their gym showers. "We do not provide soap in the showers because, God forbid, someone might slip," explained an employee of the clubhouse at Pennbroke Pines.

The Bonaventure Town Center has already paid out $50,000 to settle just one such claim after a resident slipped in the shower and filed suit. Consequently, the clubhouse has removed all soap from its showers and is now posting signs warning bathers not to bring their own. "What will be good is that we'll document the people using soap so if they slip, they'll know that they ignored the warnings. That won't look good in a jury's eye," said a club employee.

When Only the Lawyers Win

Clogging the system with frivolous claims is bad enough. Even worse are the cases in which plaintiffs have suffered genuine injury and access the legal system for redress but, thanks to their lawyers, come away empty-handed. Take the case of the non-smoking airline flight attendants who in 1998 filed a class-action suit against the tobacco companies, claiming injuries caused by exposure to secondhand smoke while working. Their attorneys negotiated them a doozy of a settlement: The lawyers got $49 million in fees, and all the flight attendants got was a study to be financed by the tobacco industry.

Reacting to this outcome, U.S. Chamber of Commerce president Tom Donohue said, "Wherever one stands on the merits of this particular case, its outcome illustrates the fact that America's civil justice system has fallen into serious disrepair. The vast majority of the nearly one million lawyers in America have been tainted by the highjacking of the legal system by a relatively small number of plaintiff's attorneys who have poured millions of dollars into the political system and transformed America into the lawsuit capital of the world."

Donohue estimates that the tort system costs consumers and businesses an estimated $160 billion every year—$2,400 for a family of four. "The cost of litigation is built into everything we buy," Donohue says. "Even worse, the fear of litigation retards the development and testing of new products, including potentially life-saving drugs and medical devices."

And the case of those flight attendants' empty pockets is hardly an isolated one. "Even more of a disgrace is the fact that less than half the money transferred through the tort system ever reaches the plaintiffs. An estimated 54 percent goes to their lawyers."

As Donohue noted, those flight attendants are not alone. According to the Institute for Legal Reform:

o   In one case over mislabeled computer monitors, the plaintiffs' lawyers were awarded $5.8 million in legal fees and up to $250,000 in expenses. Their clients received rebate forms for $6 in cash or a $13 coupon toward the purchase of a new monitor.

○ In an airline passenger case, the lawyers walked away with $16 million in fees while the passengers got $25 coupons for future air travel.

○ In a case involving a dispute over escrow fees, the settlement called for the bank to deposit a maximum of $8.76 into each class member's account—but then subtract as much as $100 to pay the lawyers' fees!

And if no victims—real or alleged—come forward, some lawyers simply go out and find them. For example, if you're a user of a Microsoft product such as its ubiquitous Windows system, an enterprising law firm may soon inform you that you are a "victim"! When a federal judge ruled that Microsoft had acted in monopolistic ways, the *Washington Post*, not normally a defender of big business, tells us what happened next in a December 2, 1999, editorial:

Barely had the ink dried on Judge Thomas Penfield Jackson's findings of fact in the Microsoft antitrust trial when plaintiff's lawyers began filing class actions against the software giant. One could hardly ask for a better portrait of everything that is predatory about class action plaintiff's lawyers. Cases such as this have next to nothing to do with the interests of consumers but are essentially commercial ventures within the judiciary. The purported clients are little more than fictions designed to legitimize the enrichment of their self-appointed representatives.

49

The newspaper goes on to report that Microsoft is hardly the first target of these legal predators.

> Five of the country's biggest HMOs were sued by lawyers claiming to represent 32 million of their customers . . . Indeed the lawyers have been recently peddling their suit around Wall Street in a deliberate attempt to depress the companies' stock value and thereby pressure them to settle. This isn't law. It's an extortion racket.

Even more disturbing is the increasing degree to which government is now joining this racket. The Clinton administration has sued the tobacco industry. Several California cities have sued gun manufacturers. Rhode Island has sued paint companies. In these cases, private sector trial lawyers have coached or teamed up with government lawyers to target legal but perhaps politically incorrect industries for huge lawsuits. The plaintiff's lawyers hope to pocket huge fees and garner publicity that will help generate future business. The government agencies hope to fill government coffers in an era when the public sees no need for tax increases. They also want to change those industries' behavior, practices, and products. Having failed to convince legislative bodies to mandate those changes, these agencies hope to accomplish their goals in the courtroom—thus bypassing the democratic process.

However one feels about those particular industries, it's troubling to see government with its unlimited resources and long legal reach team up with predatory attorneys to attack legal businesses. "Who's next?" is the question we should all be asking. Nursing homes, the gaming industry, drug companies, chemical companies, and many others may soon find themselves in the line of fire.

Fearing runaway juries rendering emotionally driven verdicts, companies and municipalities are often pressured into settling even the flimsiest of cases before they go to trial. Or, they suspend an activity just to prevent possible lawsuits in the future. ABC news correspondent John Stossel has investigated America's litigation explosion and its impact on society: "We used to have twenty companies making vaccines," he reports. "Now we have four. Fresno, California, stopped volunteers from cleaning streets because of their fear of lawsuits. You don't have honest job references anymore. You can't have honest conversations in the workplace for fear of lawsuits.

"They [lawsuits] aren't great things that solve problems. They are trashy, horrible, privacy-invading, money-eating machines that we ought to minimize, not maximize," Stossel says.

Four Standards of Justice

The Washington-based Institute for Legal Reform has evaluated our civil justice system on four standards—efficiency, timeliness, predictability, and fairness—and the system today fails each test. According to the Institute:

Efficiency: The costs of the U.S. tort system rose at a rate four times faster than national economic growth from the 1930s to the mid-1980s. Today, at a price tag of some $160 billion, the tort system costs two-and-a-half times what we spend on police and fire protection.

Timeliness: A study by the federal government's General Accounting Office showed that the average plaintiff must wait two and a half years from the moment of filing until the verdict. A study by the American Medical Association found an average delay for a medical liability claim of between two and five years. By allowing the courts to become clogged with frivolous claims, we leave genuine victims waiting years for redress.

Predictability: A recent Rand study found that jury verdicts for cases with similar facts vary dramatically across jurisdictions. And legal scholar Ted Olson, testifying before the U.S. Senate, observed: "Because there are no reliable guidelines anywhere for appropriate levels of punitive damages, when judges substitute their instincts for the jury, the results can be just as capricious, unpredictable, and inconsistent. A judge may decide on a $4 million punishment rather than $8 million, or $2 million rather than $4 million. But there's no rhyme, reason, or rationality to these decisions."

Fairness: Some litigants (and their lawyers) win big, while others with identical claims come away empty-handed. Rather than providing just compensation for those with real injuries, the tort system allows some litigants to receive a windfall while precluding others from recovering anything at all. And because liability is not tied to fault, the system is also unfair to defendants.

What Do the Lawyers Say?

When confronted with evidence that our justice system is too costly, too slow, and too litigious—and that it is largely inaccessible to Middle America, bestowing its greatest rewards on the rich and their attorneys—what does the legal establishment have to say? Unfortunately, not much—and this lack of leadership has damaged the standing of what should be viewed by the public as a great and noble profession.

In the arena of public policy, trade associations and lobbyists for the legal profession are among the most powerful groups in Washington, D.C., and the state capitals. For the most part, they use that power to block even modest reforms that would weed out the frivolous cases and rein in the excessive awards and fees. Because they are at loggerheads with an equally powerful interest—corporate America—that seeks change for both legitimate and selfish reasons, the lawmakers caught in the middle have been in a state of gridlock on legal reform issues for decades. The losers are the average citizens who simply want a fair hearing, an honest judgment, and reasonable redress for true injury in a timely fashion.

As for the lack of access to the system, the typical answer one hears from the American Bar Association and other professional societies is more pro bono work. Yet how many lawyers can really get excited about that? While important and honorable, relying on pro bono work to address the tremendous lack of access to justice in America today just nibbles around the edges. Even if lawyers wanted to do more work for free, they can't. The legal *profession* may exalt it, but the legal *business* disdains it.

Now when it comes to economics, I'm a true believer in the law of supply and demand. But when it comes to the administration of justice, here's the problem: We've got plenty of demand (actual and potential cases and the need for counsel) and plenty of supply (lawyers), yet an overwhelming share of the supply is going to meet a small fraction of the demand.

We're the most lawyered society on earth and yet tens of millions of people routinely go without legal representation. With the United States having just 5 percent of the world's population, the ABA conservatively estimates that we've got some 35 percent of the lawyers—nearly one million and counting!

I know many fine people in the legal profession, so it's kind of sad to see lawyers as a group treated with such scorn and ridicule. There are at least twenty Web sites on the Internet devoted exclusively to lawyer jokes. Shakespeare's famous line "The first thing we do is kill all the lawyers" was a message recently seen adorning a T-shirt, and the item no doubt sold briskly in shopping malls across the country.

In a more serious vein, the ABA's recent public opinion survey found that the American people hold lawyers in terribly low regard. When respondents were asked how much confidence they had in the nation's most vital institutions, lawyers ranked below every other category of professional—except for those in the media!

Just 14 percent said they had strong confidence in the legal profession; 42 percent had slight or no confidence at all. "Lawyers are often perceived to be more concerned with their own interests than [with] the public's or the clients'," the report concludes.

Many attorneys feel the same sense of frustration and disappointment as the public at large. I now talk regularly with hundreds of lawyers, and I'm convinced that most of them enter the profession with great ideals.

> We're the most lawyered society on earth and yet tens of millions of people routinely go without legal representation.

They emerge from law school determined to breathe new life into Lincoln's exhortation that reverence for the law should become "the political religion" of our nation and America should deliver on its promise of equal justice.

But then they run head-on into reality. Law is not a profession, it's a business. Justice is not a right, it's a commodity. There is cutthroat competition for clients—clients who can pay. The legal business has little if any interest in those who cannot. The aspiring lawyer who spends too much time worrying about those who cannot won't get very far. The high incomes, the lucrative partnerships, and the coveted invitations to join the top firms will go instead to those who have learned that in today's legal culture, Billable Hours Are King!

It's a sad turn of events for a profession that is so essential to our free society and that is filled with so many talented and honorable men and women. But as you will soon see, when outstanding lawyers are given an opportunity to serve the public and provide everyday Americans with equal justice in an approach that is economically viable, they will jump at the chance.

A Few Good Questions

The careful reader may think he or she has detected a contradiction in my discussion thus far. In the previous chapter, I lamented that millions of Americans were either unable to afford access to lawyers, courts, and the justice system—or that they don't know how to. Our nation will not be able to keep its promise of equal justice under law unless and until we find a way to open the system to them.

Yet in this chapter I observed that America is already awash in lawyers and litigation and that restraint and reform are in order.

So you may be wondering: Why would a man whose company and its profits are built on selling legal services find fault with our litigious culture?

Won't Pre-Paid Legal's approach of providing Americans who perhaps have never hired a lawyer before with unlimited legal consultation only add more gunpowder to this country's litigation explosion?

Or to put it another way, how come I'm not the happiest fellow in America—because everyone seems to want to sue everybody for everything?

These are good questions and there are three parts to my answer.

First, by giving Americans access to unlimited legal consultation, many lawsuits can be prevented, because our provider lawyers can steer them away from decisions that could invite those lawsuits. As you'll see when I tell you more about our products in the next chapter, *prevention* is our watchword in much of the legal work we provide for our members.

Second, the very fact that we are an extremely litigious society is proof positive that all Americans should be armed with the protective tools to defend themselves should they become the target of a frivolous or serious legal assault. It's not just the big corporations with their deep pockets that find themselves under attack. Go back and glance once more at the 101 reasons for legal protection I listed in chapter 2. Average people with pretty shallow pockets can find themselves in the dock as well.

Third, remember the words of Harvard's Dr. Derek Bok: "There is far too much law for those who can afford it and far too little for those who cannot." A nation whose courts are clogged with frivolous cases and whose best lawyers are preoccupied with the wealthiest accounts or with hitting the jackpot in specious class-action lawsuits will not have much time or attention for the rest of us.

> All Americans should be armed with the protective tools to defend themselves should they become the target of a frivolous or serious legal assault. It's not just the big corporations with their deep pockets that find themselves under attack.

By costing too much, by taking too long, by favoring the rich, by feeding on the ignorance of many about their rights, and by suppressing the best instincts in the legal profession while bringing out the worst—justice in America is failing to live up to its promise.

We have two choices for fixing it. We can wait for the politicians and the legal profession to do it. Or we can embrace an innovative, market-based idea that has gained the enthusiastic support of hundreds of thousands of clients and lawyers and that leading authorities say is already changing the face of justice in America.

Since I'm sixty-one now, I'd rather not wait for the politicians and the legal establishment. There's a much better way. It's called Pre-Paid Legal.

Chapter 4

KEEPING THE PROMISE: THE PRE-PAID LEGAL CONCEPT

Let's play a little game of "what if?"

What if you were my attorney and I called you up and told you that I wanted to work out a flat monthly fee to protect myself, my wife, and my two children—one of whom is a teenage driver—from all potential legal issues and needs that might arise.

First, I want to be able to pick up the phone and talk with you about any legal matter, personal or business. Of course, I will only call you during normal business hours.

Second, when we need anything of a personal legal nature such as a letter written, a phone call made, or a contract reviewed, we would want you to do that for us, too.

Third, I also want you to draft my will. Then each year, I would like you to review it and update it for me as needed.

Fourth, I want to have this access throughout the United States. If I'm traveling in another state and need legal advice, I expect you to refer me to an attorney in that state. That attorney should bill you, not me, and I want you to pay that bill out of this monthly arrangement we set up.

One more thing: My family and I are law-abiding citizens, but you never know when circumstances could find one of us subject to an arrest or questioning by law enforcement officers. It could be a driving-related incident, an altercation in a public place, or just a misunderstanding that escalates out of control. And it could happen any time, anywhere in the country, even at 3:00 A.M.

I want to protect my family from those situations, too. I want each of us to have someone to call in such an emergency twenty-four hours a day, seven days a week.

Now let's assume your standard rate for legal counsel is only $100 an hour—and that's a pretty reasonable price in a profession where good attorneys can cost several hundred dollars an hour and up. Having heard the kind of legal service I want, you start calculating the kind of flat monthly fee you're going to charge me. But before you get a chance to finish adding up all the big numbers, I tell you what I want to pay.

How about $14.95 a month? Oh, and I'll throw in an extra buck a month for that 24/7 emergency coverage in case of arrest.

How long would it take for you to throw me out of your office?

Under normal circumstances, it could cost anywhere from $250 to $1,000 a month or more—perhaps much more—if you walked into a lawyer's office to retain him or her for the range of services I have outlined. And unless you have an existing relationship with or knowledge of the firm you are retaining, you won't really know what you are buying for all that money.

But at Pre-Paid Legal, we can absolutely guarantee a family unlimited access during normal business hours to the best lawyers in the country for $14.95 a month—and yes, a dollar more a month for emergency service should you or a family member be taken into police custody.

How is this possible?

It's just like Ray Kroc's idea for McDonald's franchises. At the time, there were plenty of people across this country who were frying up hamburgers. And if everyone enjoyed the quality, the service,

> At Pre-Paid Legal, we can absolutely guarantee a family unlimited access during normal business hours to the best lawyers in the country for $14.95 a month—and yes, a dollar more a month for emergency service should you or a family member be taken into police custody.

the consistency, the price, and the easy access of the existing hamburger stands, he would have fallen on his face. The only McDonald we'd all know today is that old farmer in the children's song.

The legal system today is not all that different from the way Ray Kroc found the hamburger business back in 1955. We've got plenty of lawyers. They're everywhere. We've got plenty of need for their services—remember that over 50 percent of us are involved in some type of legal situation right now.

But for most Americans, the quality is questionable, the customer service is bad, the consistency is uneven, the price is exorbitant, and the access is out of reach.

What Ray Kroc did was to find a way to deliver a healthful, quality product efficiently and courteously anywhere in America, and now the world, and do it cheaper than anyone else while still making himself, his investors, and his franchisees a fortune. When he did so, he didn't just change hamburgers and the restaurant business, or rejuvenate franchising and alter the entire business world; he changed society and culture. Author Tom Robbins once wrote:

> Columbus discovered America, Jefferson invented it, and Ray Kroc Big Mac'd it. It could have been an omniscient computer that provided this land with its prevailing ambiance, it might have been an irresistible new weapons system, a political revolu-

tion, an art movement, or some gene-altering drug. How wonderful that it was a hamburger!

An Idea Whose Time Has Come

Some people might think that potentially life-and-death matters of justice don't belong in the same conversation with McDonald's hamburgers. The first topic goes to the heart of our rights and freedoms as Americans, while the second goes right to our stomachs! But the McDonald's example illuminates the true nature of our problem and, more important, points us to an answer. As I've said, it's not a question of having enough laws on the books, enough lawyers, or enough need for legal counsel and representation. It's all about how to get the services to the vast majority of people who don't know the system or where to turn.

Should we be surprised that most middle-class Americans, when faced with such an exorbitant cost, will decide instead to take their chances? To ignore taking preventative steps to stay out of legal conflicts? To wait until there's an immediate need and then scramble for representation? And should we be shocked that when they hire a law firm for a one-shot deal, the firm barely gives them the time of day because they're small, short-term clients? Not at all.

But we also have to suffer the consequences.

A system that doesn't have the full participation of the people it's supposed to serve will become easily corrupted. Invite the system to ignore you and, strangely enough, it will. Neglect to tell the system your side of the story and, strangely enough, it won't hear you. Fail to stand up for your rights and, lo and behold, your rights will be trampled on. It's that simple.

What about those who react to my concerns by saying, "Harland, when people need a lawyer, they can go out and hire one. Like you said, they're everywhere!" These are the same folks who might have told Ray Kroc, "Ray, we've already got a hamburger stand in our town. There's no need or room for you." All those questioners are missing the biggest part of the picture.

What if there was a way to give legions of middle-class Americans access to the justice system when they needed it and to give them preventative legal tools to keep those needs to a minimum? What if we could find a way to do all this, thus restoring public confidence in the justice system and the legal profession, with a high-quality service at a price virtually any family can afford?

There is a way and it's called pre-paid legal protection. I'd like to tell you that I invented it, but I did not.

But then, Ray Kroc didn't invent the hamburger, either!

Werner Pfennigstorf, research attorney for the American Bar Association and an internationally recognized scholar of insurance law, explains, "In fact, legal protection insurance was introduced in Europe about seventy years ago, and over the years has become one of the most common and popular types of insurance in the market. In all of Europe, there are about 40 million policies outstanding, with a total annual premium of about $1.2 billion.

"The European experience shows that there is a need and a strong demand for the coverage [here], and there is no reason why it should not be possible to repeat or even surpass the European success in this country."

Like most Americans, I don't like to think that we're lagging behind any other country in anything! But when it comes to providing preventative legal protection and pre-paid legal service to average people, we are. It's a gap my company is fixing to close and fast!

Mr. Pfennigstorf understands this: "The formula that made legal protection insurance so successful in Europe is the same as that employed by Pre-Paid Legal Services, Inc. This company has more in common with the most successful European legal protection companies than any other American company I know.

"If anyone holds the key to duplicating the European success, this company does."

He's not the only one to note that the kind of pre-paid legal protection pioneered in America by our company is catching on. Here are a few other authoritative voices:

- *Success* magazine: "This is the wave of the future. The total legal industry for the 80 percent of Americans in the middle class is a $15 billion to $25 billion industry, and you'll see all the big insurance companies come into it. Their existing accounts will ask for it."

65

o *Black Enterprise* magazine: "The average person faces legal issues four to six times a year. There are instances where legal advice could be helpful, but most people are hesitant to talk to a lawyer because they don't feel it would be cost effective. The advantage of a legal services plan . . . is that it gives you access to information and assistance that can protect your interests."

o *Washington Business Times:* "The number of Americans covered by legal services insurance of some sort rose 10.8 percent—the largest gain in five years—to a record 98 million people last year."

o The *Orange County Register:* "Within a few years legal insurance will be as available and as common as medical coverage."

o *Business Week:* "Never mind the 401(k), how's the legal plan? More and more, prepaid legal care is taking its place alongside hot employee perks . . . with such employers as AT&T, American Express, and the Big Three auto makers."

o *Chicago Tribune:* "It is clear that what this country needs is a massive overhaul of the legal system, leading to comprehensive legal care for every American."

o The *Wall Street Journal:* "There is legal aid for the poor and private attorneys for the rich, but until now we have never had anything for the working middle class. Thanks to pre-paid legal plans, this group is finally able to afford legal services."

How do pre-paid legal plans work? The concept is simple. What we do is gather together a whole bunch of customers (whom we call members) and charge each of them a small monthly fee, for which we promise them a specific set of services. We then pool the money they pay us and use it to retain the very best law firms in the country to provide those services for our members.

Thus, individual members get a much better law firm at a much lower cost than they could ever get on their own. Law firms that probably would never give the time of day to our individual members if they called on their own, pay a great deal of attention to them because those firms have to answer to us—Pre-Paid Legal Services, Inc.—for we are one of their biggest clients, if not their biggest.

As I said, the concept is simple. And as long as I keep on telling myself this, maybe I'll forget what a struggle it has been to put into practice and gain acceptance for such a straightforward idea!

More about that later. But first, let me expand on what Pre-Paid Legal can do for the average American who until now has been left out of American justice.

The Pre-Paid Legal Products

The bottom line is that for as little as $14.95 a month, we can give people access to top-quality law firms in America. And it's not just access, it's unlimited access—

not just for you but for your entire family. Call as many times as you want during normal business hours.

And when you call, if the phone rings more than three times, that's too many. And if this happens too often, that firm gets a call from us!

I tell the people who work for our company and the independent sales associates who sell our memberships all around the country what a fantastic job they do—and it's true. But then I tell them, and continually remind myself, that it's the product above all else that explains our success. If we had not developed a product that meets such a great need and, just as important, if we had not devised a system to guarantee the quality of that product, Pre-Paid Legal Services would not be number 13 on the *Forbes* list of the fastest-growing companies or number 33 on the New York Stock Exchange list of top-performing companies. We are a product-driven company, pure and simple. Because most Americans are unfamiliar with pre-paid legal products, I'd like to describe them in some detail, along with the extensive steps we take to ensure their quality.

The Family Legal Plan

Our most popular product, the Family Legal Plan, consists of five basic benefits (called Titles) that provide coverage for a broad range of preventative and litigation-related legal expenses for a monthly fee of $14.95–$25, depending on the services chosen. Here's what they are and what members of this plan can expect:

Title I—Preventative Legal Services

- Unlimited phone consultation: toll-free access to a provider attorney for personal or business-related legal matters.
- Phone calls and letters from a provider attorney on a member's behalf: an unlimited number of subjects, including two business letters per year.
- Contract and document review: an unlimited number of documents, up to ten pages each, including one business document per year.
- Standard will preparation: the member's will at no added charge with yearly reviews and updates. Wills for covered family members are just $20.

Title II—Motor Vehicle Legal Services

- Immediate consultation with a provider attorney upon getting a ticket.
- Representation for moving traffic violations.
- Representation for certain motor vehicle–related criminal charges.

- Up to 2.5 hours for help with driver's license assistance and personal injury/property damage collection assistance of $2,000 or less.

Title III—Trial Defense Services

- If a member or a member's spouse faces a civil suit or job-related criminal charges, the provider attorney will provide up to 75 hours to defend that person at no added cost. Additional pre-trial and trial services are available at a 25 percent discount off the attorney's standard hourly rate.
- The provider attorney will assist the member even if his or her insurance company appoints an attorney.
- The longer a membership is kept, the more hours of attorney defense services are included. For example, a five-year member receives 335 total hours of pre-trial and trial time from the provider lawyer.

Title IV—IRS Audit and Legal Services

- A total of 50 hours of attorney services, including 1 hour for consultation and advice upon receipt of a written notice from the IRS.
- Up to 2.5 hours of consultation and advice after 30 days without settlement.

○ Up to the balance of 46.5 hours for trial representation.

Title V—Other Legal Services

○ The provider attorney will render assistance at a 25 percent discount off his or her standard hourly rate for legal services not otherwise covered by the membership. And if you own a business and wish representation for that entity, you will receive a 25 percent discount off the provider attorney's corporate rate.

Now let me get a bit more specific about the services included in this, our most popular plan, so you can understand in concrete terms how preventative legal service and legal defense can protect you in today's society—just as the wealthy and powerful are served and protected by their lawyers.

Toll-Free Access—What to Expect: Pre-Paid Legal members are assigned a provider attorney in their state and are free to call a toll-free access number as many times as they need to during normal business hours. A well-trained client service representative will answer the phone and ask about the subject area of your legal question. An attorney at the firm who specializes in your area of inquiry will call you back in a timely manner. All legal consultations are provided by licensed, practicing attorneys. Your provider attorney may suggest options or let you know the steps you need to take to handle your particular legal situation.

Phone Calls and Letters—What to Expect: Although not all legal problems can be simply resolved, many members find that a phone call or letter by an attorney on their behalf is of tremendous help. Your provider attorney will recommend this course of action when he or she believes it would be helpful. Members are frequently surprised and delighted by the actions and resolutions that are prompted when the other party receives a letter on the letterhead of a top law firm.

Document Review—What to Expect: When you have questions about a written document, such as a health club membership contract, you should first call your provider attorney's toll-free number. If after consultation, you need to have an attorney review the document, he or she will do so. There is no limit to the number of personal documents, up to ten pages each, that may be renewed. In addition, the membership includes review of one business document per year.

Will Preparation—What to Expect: Considering the average billing rate of attorneys, it would not be uncommon for you to be charged well over $100 for what could be classified as a simple will. As a Pre-Paid Legal member, you are entitled to have your will prepared according to your desires at no additional charge. Any other covered person—your spouse, for example—can have a will prepared for just $20. As soon as you join Pre-Paid, the company will mail you a will questionnaire. It will then be reviewed by your provider attorney and used to prepare the legal document for your signature.

Traffic Defense—What to Expect: Fifteen days after joining Pre-Paid, should you get a ticket, don't just pay it. Call your provider attorney immediately. Traffic tickets and fines can raise the cost of your car insurance and jeopardize your driving privileges. When you need legal representation for a moving traffic violation, your provider attorney will represent you in the court of original jurisdiction at no additional charge. Court costs, fines, and related fees are your responsibility. Legal assistance is also available to help reinstate a suspended driver's license.

Traffic Accident and Damage Recovery—What to Expect: It's your worst nightmare—a traffic accident resulting in loss of life. What would you do if you were involved in a serious accident and someone was killed? Legal defense bills can range in the thousands of dollars, and costs for damages are extensive. As a Pre-Paid member, your attorney will represent you when you are criminally charged with manslaughter, involuntary manslaughter, vehicular homicide, or negligent homicide. He or she will represent you in the court of original jurisdiction at no additional charge. The plan also provides limited assistance with personal injury and property damage collection. Court costs, fines, and related fees are your responsibility and DUI/DWI–related matters, drug-related matters, and hit and run–related charges are covered only under Title I.

Trial Defense—What to Expect: Legal assistance is available to help defend you or your spouse against civil suits—such as those filed by a disgruntled neighbor or a person injured on your property, claiming negligence on your part. Job-related criminal charges are also covered.

IRS Audit Services—What to Expect: A Pre-Paid Legal membership will help defray the legal-related expenses that occur when the IRS comes a-calling! Schedule C, corporate, and business tax returns are not included.

Preferred Member Discount—What to Expect: A provider attorney will render assistance at 25 percent less than his or her normal fees for services not covered by the Pre-Paid Legal membership. Many members find this a valuable benefit because for the first time they have developed a rapport and a trusting relationship with a top law firm. They become premium clients of that firm, thanks to Pre-Paid's standing as one of its biggest customers. We make sure that the 25 percent discount is a true hourly discount from the usual fees charged. In some cases, we have even arranged for contingency fee reductions of 3 to 5 percent when permissible by law.

The Legal Shield

What would you do if you were detained by a law enforcement officer for an expired driver's license? Alleged theft? Or if you were involved in a fatal auto accident? Or maybe you believe you've been unfairly targeted and detained because of your age, gender, or race?

Do you know what your rights are if this happens? What would you do if you found yourself in this sort of situation at 1:00 A.M. on a Saturday morning? Would you know whom to call? If you happen to have a lawyer, do you know his or her home phone number? Do you really think this lawyer would welcome your call?

These issues and the disturbing frequency with which citizens are being unfairly detained and inappropriately treated have prompted our company to add an important legal service to our package—for the price of one additional dollar per month.

We call it the Legal Shield program—and it gives you access to a quality lawyer twenty-four hours a day, seven days a week, for those kinds of emergencies. As a Legal Shield participant you get a little card to carry around in your wallet, purse, or glove compartment. It states:

> *This person is a member of the Legal Shield program and has 24-hour access to legal representation by a law firm provided by Pre-Paid Legal Services, Inc., and its subsidiaries. To any law enforcement or security personnel: If it is your intention to question, detain, or arrest me, please allow me to call an attorney immediately.*

Members of the program who are detained or arrested are advised to show this card and then place a collect call to the number listed on the card. The call rings at our offices in Ada, and if the member's criteria meet the plan's requirements, we call a provider attorney on the spot—sometimes even conferencing the lawyer in on the member's call to answer questions and provide advice. If additional services are needed, they will be provided at a 25 percent discount unless they fall under another area of the Family Plan membership package.

James Merritt, Jr., one of our provider attorneys, understands how important this new legal protection can be. "Perhaps no other Constitutional right is as well known to the public at large as the Miranda rights," he tells us. "Yet I believe that no other right is so frequently waived by those who need it the most.

"Hardened criminals assert their Miranda rights arrogantly. Ordinary citizens, however, are usually so traumatized by the experience of an arrest that they often waive their Miranda rights. Whether this waiver occurs from sheer panic or a fearful desire to make friends with an intimidating officer doesn't matter. Once waived, the honest citizen loses his or her best protection against a life-shattering conviction."

The purpose of the Legal Shield card is not to use it defiantly or arrogantly, but to use it politely to exercise your rights. We don't have to change the laws. All we have to do is give people access to them. With the Legal Shield we are offering people a benefit that even the rich don't have. After all, how many of them can call their personal lawyer at home at 3 A.M.?

We direct our core package of services at individuals and their families, marketing it to them either one-on-one or through group sales at their place of work as an employee option or benefit. Yet we have also devised plans for several groups of Americans with distinct needs for specialized legal services and protection—peace officers, commercial drivers, and business owners.

Law Officers Legal Plan

As I've said, I can't imagine anyone in this country with a tougher job than the men and women of law enforcement. And even though I've cited a number of situations where citizens must protect themselves from the human shortcomings and institutional flaws of law enforcement officers, I firmly believe that all but a handful of cops carry out their duties with great courage and professionalism. And their reward is frequently to be unfairly targeted or falsely accused by lawbreakers trying to get off the hook.

In approximately half the states, we offer a special Law Officers Legal Plan for peace officers and their families. The services include:

- twenty-four-hour toll-free telephone access to a provider attorney in emergency situations
- toll-free consultation for personal and business advice
- phone calls and letters made on the member's behalf
- will preparation
- contract and document review
- administrative and termination hearing representation
- trial defense services
- tragic accident representation
- IRS audit legal services
- 25 percent discount on other legal services not specifically covered

Commercial Drivers Legal Plan

Even in our Internet economy, most of the 3 trillion dollars' worth of consumer goods moving around the American marketplace annually all begins and ends in a truck. Even though 70 percent of the accidents involving a car and a truck are determined to be the car driver's fault, commercial drivers often find themselves the target of blame and with a costly need to defend their record and their continued livelihood.

We have developed products for the millions of drivers who move our economy. The Basic Commercial Drivers Legal Plan provides tragic accident representation, moving violation representation, license reinstatement services, Department of Transportation and non-moving violation representation, property damage and personal injury collection, and a 25 percent reduction on all other legal services.

The more expansive Road America CDLP offers those benefits as well as bail bond service, arrest bond service, legal and roadside services when driving personal vehicles, and travel discounts.

Business Owners Legal Solutions Plan

Perhaps no other group of Americans can become so quickly overwhelmed by legal issues due to a lack of knowledge and a lack of legal protection. I know—I've been there.

The Business Owners Legal Solutions Plan provides small businesses with comprehensive services such as:

o toll-free legal consultations
o letters and phone calls made on behalf of the business
o contract and document review

- initial debt collection letters
- trial defense services for civil actions related to business activities
- reduced service fees

In addition to these services, small business members may take advantage of the benefits provided by the Fran Tarkenton Small Business NETwork—a dynamic community of entrepreneurs committed to helping small firms grow and have access to goods and services at reduced prices.

The plan is available to privately held for-profit companies with fewer than 100 employees. It costs $75 per month for firms with less than 50 workers and $125 per month for those with 50 to 99 employees.

A Passion for Quality and Service

We have devised creative products that meet a real need, products that are revolutionizing the American legal system and keeping the promise of equal justice. But without extraordinary steps to guarantee the quality of the legal counsel and the manner in which it is delivered, we would at best be spinning our wheels and at worst, we'd collapse. In fact, if we wanted to find the one way to guarantee the Pre-Paid Legal concept almost instant extinction, there would be a simple way to do it—fall down on quality or fail on service.

This is a tremendous challenge for any company in the pre-paid legal field, a challenge made all the more daunting by two realities:

First, the concept only works if the price stays within reach of the average American. That means we must reach critical mass in terms of the number of clients in order to finance contracts with top-quality lawyers.

Second, with lawyers we are dealing with professionals who are notoriously bad at customer service—or what the doctors would call "bedside manner." That assessment will not come as a surprise or an insult to most lawyers. I've had dozens tell me that themselves.

> If we wanted to find the one way to guarantee the Pre-Paid Legal concept almost instant extinction, there would be a simple way to do it—fall down on quality or fail on service.

And so we have established the most stringent quality controls and services practices, and we have employed high technology to track, enforce, and control the kind of service we want and expect our provider law firms to provide.

It all begins with the choice of law firms. Leslie Fisher, a sixteen-year veteran of Pre-Paid Legal and currently attorney response manager for the company, deserves much of the credit for developing the provider system we have in place today.

"Provider law firms are chosen for each state based on a number of factors," she explains, "including recommendations from other attorneys, our own investigation of bar association standing, and client references. We also evaluate the education, experience, and areas of practice of attorneys within the firm and we make on-site visits to see if the firm has or can quickly acquire the culture of customer service that we insist upon.

"The vast majority of the firms are 'AV' rated by Martindale-Hubbell, the highest rating possible. Martindale-Hubbell has maintained ratings for the legal community for over a century, drawing upon the confidential opinions of judges and other lawyers as to the abilities and ethics of the lawyers in a particular firm in order to rate them.

"Each member of the provider attorney firm rendering services must have at least two years of experience as an attorney, except in some very special cases."

Leslie's last point is particularly significant because other companies in the legal protection industry make no bones about the fact that they are saving money by having non-lawyers or very junior ones provide the services. We just won't do that—and while I should be pleased by the competitive advantage our company gains as a result, in fact I'm not. Our success in changing the legal system in America depends so heavily on the confidence people have in the quality of counsel they can receive from pre-paid legal service plans. Shortcuts by some companies make our task that much harder.

I don't have anything against paralegals or new lawyers. We all had to start at one time or another with no experience. But think about how you'd feel if you went into the hospital to have open-heart surgery and your doctor walks in and says, "This is a big day. You're my very first open-heart operation!" I don't know about you, but I'd be really concerned.

We ought to feel the same way about lawyers. I want mine to have some experience. It's easy to say that a particular family's legal problem isn't such a big deal. But as I've noted, for that family at that particular time it's the biggest deal in the world. It ought to be treated like a big deal by a big-time law firm.

Those are the kind of lawyers we have and that's the kind of service we demand.

What Our Lawyers Look Like

Leslie outlined the rigorous procedures we go through to select our provider firms. But who's to say that the top firms will want to work for Pre-Paid Legal? How do we land them and put them to work for average Americans who have little to spend on legal service?

We use a secret weapon called—money! Pooling the small monthly fees of more than 800,000 member clients buys us a lot of clout in the legal community. We pay firms on a per capita basis, based on the number of members in a given state. Since our members use the services differently and with varying degrees of frequency, it's a good deal for the law firms. In a number of cases, Pre-Paid Legal is their biggest customer. One provider attorney told us, "It's like doing pro bono work, except I get paid for it." Another simply marveled: "Harland, first you make my phone ring and then you pay me for it!"

People who question or don't understand the quality of the firms we have engaged need a little schooling in the economies of scale. Surprisingly (or maybe not!), I've run into some folks in the financial markets on Wall Street who have the biggest problem with this concept.

> Pooling the small monthly fees of more than 800,000 member clients buys us a lot of clout in the legal community.

In fact, when I first started going to Wall Street to brief investors on Pre-Paid Legal, some of them looked at me the way they must have first looked at Ray Kroc when he told them he was going to build a global corporate empire on the basis of what were then fifteen-cent hamburgers.

One analyst even asked me, "Tell me, Mr. Stonecipher, what do these $15-a-month lawyers look like?"

When I returned to Oklahoma, I had a chat with Mike Turpen, a former state attorney general and now a member of our provider law firm. I said, "Mike, those fellows in New York wanted to know what our $15-a-month attorneys look like."

"Harland," he replied, "Next time they ask you that, tell them I look like a million bucks—because that's what you paid me last year!"

That was six years ago. This year we'll pay Mike Turpen's firm $3 million. Now, Mike's a big-time lawyer and few of us walking in off the street could afford to hire him. But $3 million a year from Pre-Paid gets his attention! The same goes for our provider firms in other states. In Texas, for example, we sent our firm there $750,000 last month. Before long, we'll be paying some of our firms $1 million a month. There's not a law firm in this country whose attention you can't get for $1 million a month!

That's what our "$15-a-month" lawyers look like!

High-Tech Quality Control

But money alone doesn't guarantee quality and superior service. There are a lot of products and services we pay high prices for in this country on the basis of reputation and image, not reality. We're making sure Pre-Paid Legal's products and services don't fall into that category. It's what really distinguishes us from other legal service companies.

I wish you could see the back room of our headquarters building in Ada. You'd think you just stepped into the *Starship Enterprise*. It's full of high-tech computer stations and monitoring equipment to track and oversee the work and responsiveness of our provider attorneys. I'll be honest with you, I don't precisely know down to last bit and byte how it all works. I just know it does work—and it costs plenty to make it work!

Every day, Leslie Fisher and I get a computerized report on our desks that tells us how many calls members made to each provider law firm. We find out how many rings it took for the phone to be picked up and how long it took before an attorney called the member back with an answer, a suggestion, or a solution. For every call that comes in, we have staff in Ada following its course, from initial inquiry to final disposition. Naturally, we survey members frequently and investigate each complaint thoroughly.

In doing so, we strive to be tough but fair. Tough, in that law firms that fall below our severe standards are warned and, on a few occasions, replaced. Fair, in that we recognize that in many cases, a member's complaint is driven by the fact that he or she didn't get the hoped-for results, not because the service fell short.

To those who say we are constantly looking over our lawyers' shoulders, the simple answer is—yes. But we never interfere with or violate the attorney-client privilege. To those who grumble that even so, our quality controls are too intrusive, the blunt answer is—that's too bad. That's the way it's got to be.

Virtually all of our attorneys discover that our quality controls and near-obsession with customer service round out an important part of their training. And that is how to provide clients with helpful, courteous, efficient, and comforting service.

Lawyers don't learn these important values in law school, and the profession as a whole has suffered for it. I'm proud that our focus on customer service is changing the culture of the legal profession and closing an important gap between lawyer and client.

Three Cheers from Three Lawyers

Few things after thirty years in this business are more rewarding than seeing lawyers discover how wonderful it can be to help everyday people solve their problems and to be thanked and rewarded for doing so.

I first met John Lisle in 1986. He was working for a Little Rock, Arkansas, law firm that I was trying to interest in becoming a provider firm for Pre-Paid.

I wasn't doing a very good job. There wasn't much interest at all. Neither John nor his partners had ever heard of Pre-Paid Legal. So I just laid out some simple arithmetic, telling them how many members we had in Arkansas and what we would pay for each one. Just call me if you're interested, I told them.

"None of my partners were interested," John recalls. "I told them that Harland Stonecipher either doesn't have a clue as to what he's doing or he's come up with the best deal in the world. Let's give it a try!"

John's senior partner basically told him, "Well, if you're so interested, then you can be the one to handle it." And so he did!

"Getting involved with Pre-Paid Legal has changed my career and my life," John says. "Before Pre-Paid, I had done as much pro bono work as I could for twenty years. But there's a myth about pro bono legal work. When a lawyer does it, it's not just that he's refusing to charge for it. In a sense he's actually paying out money because there are costs involved, the biggest one being the use of what is really a finite supply of the lawyer's time.

"Pre-Paid solves that problem by allowing us to do enormously satisfying work—the kind of satisfaction we get from pro bono cases—but still get paid for it."

The rewards didn't come overnight. "Back in 1986 things moved pretty slowly," John continues. "The state of Arkansas made things difficult in a regulatory sense. But by 1989, it was really blasting off. I moved my firm to Springdale, Arkansas—right in the heart of the prosperous and more modern part of our state. I designed a brand new office building with computers and a phone system specifically to service Pre-Paid members. We've got eight attorneys working on it full-time—and two of them are my sons! We all love the work. Our philosophy is that if Pre-Paid comes up with a new idea or technique to provide better service, we'll give it a try.

"I think the company is making us better lawyers. Pre-Paid is completely changing our culture. Now our

The house I grew up in. There was no electricity or indoor plumbing in that house, but plenty of love and support.

My parents, Allen and Viola Stonecipher. They worked in the fields every day and never complained.

Graduating from high school in 1956. None of my siblings finished high school. My dad always insisted that I would.

Wedding day, August 22, 1958.
I was 20 years old, and Shirley
was 18. Forty-two years later,
we still feel like newlyweds!

The first college graduate in the
Stonecipher family. Me graduating
from East Central State University in
Ada, Oklahoma, 1960.

Shirley and I celebrating my college degree.
Finishing school and becoming a teacher
were my dad's biggest dreams for me.

The car accident that started it all. My brush with disaster on July 11, 1969, and the legal problems that followed gave me the idea for Pre-Paid Legal.

Mr. and Mrs. Nick Pope. Nick was president and founder of National Foundation Life Insurance Company and one of the most important mentors in my life.

Charlie and Laverne Walls, great friends and business associates. It was Charlie who convinced me to leave teaching for business. Then he became my teacher in the field of sales.

Wilburn Smith and Rick Haney at a Pre-Paid Legal sales meeting in Ada in the early 1980s. Rick, who passed away at an early age, was the most enthusiastic salesman I've ever known. I still keep his briefcase in my office to remind me what courage, character, and hard work are all about. Today Wilburn is president of our company.

John and Helen Hail saved Pre-Paid Legal from bankruptcy more than once and introduced us to the power and promise of network marketing.

Shirley and I with sons Brent and Allen. I'm so proud that they graduated from the same schools as me and still live nearby. They're both successful businessmen in their own right.

Our home for the past 24 years— just 10 miles south of where I grew up.

I surprised Shirley one Christmas with this yellow Mercedes SLK Sports Coupe. Shirley grew up much like I did, and this is about the only indulgence she has accepted from our business success.

Graduations are a big deal in the Stonecipher family. Here's grandson Greg graduating from kindergarten. His parents, Karen and Allen, brother Zane, and cousin Nikki join Shirley and me in celebration.

Brent with wife, Tina, and daughter, Nikki, during
one of our annual Pre-Paid Legal Christmas
retreats in Branson, Missouri.

Our grandchildren, Greg, Nikki, and Zane. At Pre-Paid Legal,
we're working to make America a better and fairer
place for them and all children.

Wilburn and Carol Smith. There's hardly a job that Wilburn hasn't done at Pre-Paid Legal over the past 20 years. He did all of them so well, we made him president of the company! Our independent sales force respects Wilburn so much because he has "been there—done that."

Shirley and I stealing away for a moment of peace and quiet during a meeting of our top sales associates in Jackson Hole, Wyoming.

Shirley, me, and Lady Justice taking center stage at our recent national convention in Dallas. "Equal Justice Under Law" is more than a slogan to me. It's a life mission.

Speaking at our 1999 Pre-Paid Christmas trip to Branson. I took speech and debate courses back in college because I was afraid to stand up in front of people and talk. Now I make hundreds of speeches and presentations a year.

Shirley and me at our 1999 convention in Tulsa, Oklahoma. Without Shirley's love, support and wise counsel, Pre-Paid Legal would not exist today.

Ringing the bell at the New York Stock Exchange the day Pre-Paid Legal Services Inc. started trading there, May 13, 1999. Sharing the moment are Peter Grunebaum, Eric Worre, Ron Diaz, William R. Johnston, me, Shirley, Jeff Olson, Tom Smith, and Randy Harp. Wall Street is a long way from Coal County, Oklahoma, for this son of sharecroppers!

bottom line is to make the callers feel better about their problems—and many of the calls aren't really even legal questions."

But many are—and John Lisle is proud of the cases where, for their small monthly Pre-Paid Legal fees, members, just average people with no real clout or connections, were able to access the legal system and save many thousands of dollars.

"One case involved a woman who had cancer. She had over $100,000 in unpaid medical bills that her insurance company refused to cover because it said they were for experimental treatment. One of our attorneys read the fine print in her health plan and found they should be covered. We got her bill paid in full!

"If that woman had come in off the street to another law firm, chances are they would have taken her case on a contingency basis—and collected $33,000 as a fee when the case was won!" John explains.

Another Pre-Paid Legal member living in a small town 250 miles from the Lisles' home office found that he was being foreclosed for not paying his mortgage. John explains:

"He had borrowed $20,000 to be paid over twenty years. After making timely payments for twenty years and nine months, the man figured it was more than paid off and stopped sending in the checks. The bank foreclosed because it claimed nothing in the note said it would be paid off in twenty years and in fact, it had amortized the note over thirty years.

"We won in court, got the foreclosure dismissed, and saved his home."

Despite these and many other victorious cases for Pre-Paid members, John says it is the service that pleases people the most.

"We have attorneys who do nothing but work the phones—and by the way, some lawyers like working the regular business hours we're supposed to be covering those phones. They get to balance their family priorities with a rewarding legal career.

"Every survey I've ever seen about lawyers shows that the public's number one complaint is that lawyers don't return their phone calls. Our clients love the fact that they can actually get attorneys on the phone!

"Perhaps the most important thing Pre-Paid Legal has done is introduce the concept of service to the legal business. You have to gear your whole office around the company's requirements. And not only that, you're constantly evaluated—and the thing we and other Pre-Paid lawyers dreaded the most at first was that they would actually survey the members to see how satisfied they were with our service. Typically, lawyers absolutely hate it when the clients are asked how we did. But Pre-Paid provider attorneys can get pretty pumped up by it."

Ron Glantz, our provider attorney in South Florida, echoes many of John Lisle's views and emphasizes that lawyers' legendary lack of customer service is not the only hurdle keeping Middle America away from the justice system—so does the cost. Ron has been an advocate of the Pre-Paid Legal concept at least as long as I have, serving in the early 1980s with the national Pre-Paid Legal Institute, a group dedicated to advancing the idea of legal protection for average citizens. What he has been waiting for is someone to come along and do it right!

"It's a wonderful vehicle to give people access to attorneys whom they otherwise could not afford. It's not much more complicated than that," Ron explains. "Not only do you feel very good about yourself and the work you are doing, the economics make a lot of sense, too.

"There's a lot of lawyers out there, a lot of competition. Many may get to charge $125 an hour and up—but they're only busy twenty hours a week. Why not be busy all the time at a lower rate per client and do more good things for people?" Ron asks.

"We get letters every day from members thanking us for what we've done. Frankly, other law firms who used to look down on the concept are now kind of jealous that they're not involved in it. The acceptance is growing by the day. You're finally seeing bar associations and courts weighing in favor of it because it creates access to the legal system for people who have been left out."

Like John Lisle, Ron emphasizes the need for customer service and strict quality control. "It's absolutely crucial, especially with lawyers," he says. "What distinguishes this company from others in the field is the focus on providing service. We are online and interconnected with Pre-Paid's home office.

"You have to understand that many lawyers have an attitude that says, 'I'm a lawyer and I'm better than you.' You come down to earth when you represent Pre-Paid Legal members and you rediscover that your true job as a lawyer is to help people."

Another provider attorney, Sid Friedman of Maryland, explains that what attracts him the most to the prepaid legal approach is that "it gives service to the middle class, which has been basically ignored by the bar for the last hundred years.

"I'm just amazed at the pent-up demand for preventative law that Pre-Paid Legal has untapped. We can get eight hundred calls in our office on any given Monday, which never would have happened if it were not for Pre-Paid. Most of them are just seeking some consultation and guidance and they're satisfied simply to be talking to an expert. We relieve a lot of anxiety and that's a very important role of the legal profession that has been overlooked by the traditional bar," Sid explains.

Most legal issues, according to Sid, shouldn't have to involve spending hundreds if not thousands of dollars and all the time it takes for meetings. "Just yesterday, I had a small business member call me up to see what I thought of a joint venture contract he was about to sign with another firm. I told him it was way off the mark. He replied, 'I thought so but I wasn't sure.' Then together we made some notes about what a good agreement should look like and he went back to his potential partner with that. To me, that kind of helpfulness and problem solving is what being a lawyer is all about.

"And let me be honest with you about something that will stay in my mind forever. I've been practicing for twenty-five years—and for the first twenty, until I got involved with Pre-Paid, I represented businesses and I don't remember ever getting a thank-you letter or a real heartfelt expression of appreciation.

"But in 1995, just after Pre-Paid Legal was really getting rolling in Maryland, I got a call from a member, an Asian-American woman who told me in very broken English that she had a tenant who wasn't paying the rent. 'You send letter—make her pay,' she told me. I sent the letter and a month later, my client called me and said, 'Tenant pay—me very happy.'

"Then about six months after that, the company sponsored a huge meeting at the University of Maryland campus in College Park. There were thousands of people in the auditorium and crowding the lobby. In the midst of the noise and confusion I heard my name and it was the woman, standing there with ten family members. She said they had come to thank me and had arranged a lunch in my honor for solving their problem!

"Harland, you and Shirley were there that day and I remember telling Shirley afterward that in twenty-five years of practicing law, that was the nicest fee I ever got."

Sid strongly believes that the changes we're making in the system will affect the entire legal profession, not just the attorneys who join our provider group. "Pre-Paid Legal is changing the way legal services are being delivered," he says. "And what happens as more and more people realize there's no reason to be paying hundreds of dollars an hour for lawyers? The ones who don't change will become dinosaurs, feeding off a changed environment. It's no accident that you see many lawyers signing up for the plan themselves!

"Just because you're paying $400 an hour doesn't mean you're buying the best. Besides, you don't always need to pay top dollar to get your problem solved. You can easily throw too much lawyering at a relatively simple problem. All you're doing is wasting your money.

"At age fifty-two I'm enjoying being a lawyer more than I ever have because I'm helping more people than I ever have and mentoring them through their problems. And one more thing. There's no such thing in law school as a course called Courtesy 101. That's why most lawyers are so bad at it. With Pre-Paid Legal you learn it real fast."

John Lisle, Ron Glantz, and Sid Friedman are just three of many outstanding provider attorneys who have rediscovered, through Pre-Paid Legal, the true calling of their profession—and that is to help everyday people make the law work for them and to help our nation live up to its promise of equal justice for all.

They, like me, believe that after nearly three decades of building a solid, successful launching pad of products and systems, customers and providers, the Pre-Paid Legal concept is ready to blast off like a rocket. But it's been a long, hard struggle to reach this point. And when I think back to my boyhood in that small sharecropper's shack—devoid of plumbing and electricity but full of love and support—it's a miracle that we ever did.

Chapter 5

ONLY IN AMERICA

The most extraordinary thing about my story is that in America, it's not that extraordinary. Yet when Shirley and I rang the opening bell of the New York Stock Exchange on the day the company we founded started trading there, we felt very extraordinary. We almost pinched each other to make sure it wasn't all just a dream!

Where else but in America could the son of poor sharecroppers have an idea that the whole establishment opposed and, without money or connections, watch that idea take root and grow into a prosperous company—and then be the CEO of that company as it takes its place alongside General Motors and IBM on Wall Street?

It is a long way from Coal County, Oklahoma, to the New York Stock Exchange!

Only in America. But as I said, it's only extraordinary in that it happens here all the time. We are blessed to live in a country that mass-produces miracles. The opportunities are here—not for the whiners and complainers but for the doers and dreamers. I like to tell people about where I come from, not because I think I'm that special but to make sure they understand that no matter what handicaps are standing in their way, they can overcome them and succeed.

Something else is extraordinary about our country—it loves failures.

Yes, you read that right. In America, you can fail once, twice, three times, even more, and still come back and triumph. You can make mistakes and have setbacks. The world of business in particular is full of men and women who struck out several times, even went bankrupt, before they made an idea work. The only way anyone keeps from making mistakes is by doing nothing.

I know this firsthand, because I had more than my share of reversals, mistakes, and near misses at bankruptcy.

But even in America, this land of the individual, you don't do it alone. And people who say they did are fooling you and themselves. They are also failing to give credit where credit is due.

In my case I was blessed from the start with parents who may have had empty pockets but whose hearts were always filled with love.

My parents, Viola and Allen Stonecipher, were share-croppers, trying to make a living by growing peanuts and cotton on 170 acres of Coal County, Oklahoma, dirt that really wasn't good for growing much of anything. I don't think they ever took home more than $50 a month from those fields.

But they worked hard—I mean, unbelievably hard. Every day my mother got up at 5:30 A.M. to cook break-fast. Sometimes it was just biscuits and gravy left over from dinner the night before. Then it was out to the fields for both of them and me, too, if there was no school. They did that back-breaking work for five or six hours until around noon, when my mother would cook lunch. Then it was out to the fields again until the sun started to fade in the sky. I can still feel the heat and taste the dirt.

Where else but in America could the son of poor share-croppers have an idea that the whole establishment opposed and, without money or connections, watch that idea take root and grow into a prosperous company.

We lived in what was called a shotgun house. It was perched on a hill outside of the little town of Tupelo (population 365) about thirty miles from Ada. There was a small living room, a bedroom for my parents, and a kitchen. A tiny side room was later attached to the kitchen for me.

Since I was considerably younger than my four brothers and sisters, it was basically me and my folks while I grew up in that little house. We didn't have electricity, a telephone, or indoor plumbing. For water, my Dad dug two wells and it was just our luck that the water in the well closest to the house was too salty to drink. So ever since I can remember, it was my job to haul the drinking water up from the good well. Then I filled the tub in our backyard with the salty water so that the sun would warm it throughout the day. That's where my parents each bathed after a hard day in the fields. As for me, I preferred the cattle pond down at the foot of the hill—at least, during the summer!

On those hot summer nights my folks and I would sit outside and cool off. The metal roof that covered the house may have been pretty good at keeping out some of the harsher elements, but it didn't do a very good job at keeping out the Oklahoma heat. Other times we'd gather around an oil lamp where I would read the stories of Zane Grey and my parents talked until their bone-tired bodies took over and they drifted off to sleep.

It always amazed me, and does to this day, how my father kept his faith in the future. As for my mother, I never once heard her complain about her lot in life—not once.

It's beautiful country, these rolling hills of Oklahoma, but looking back at its history, a kind of sadness hangs over the land. We lived not far from the Trail of Tears, where the Cherokees marched through a killing winter to escape the advance of the white man.

Looking back, it would be easy to describe my steps into adulthood as a Trail of Tears, especially when I think about how hard my parents worked and how much they sacrificed for me—never complaining, never giving up, and never losing hope. What kept them going was their faith in the most powerful dream America has to offer—the dream that the future will always outshine the past and that our children will always lead a better life than our own.

But it really wasn't as bad as the descriptions of it may seem. As poor as we were, I remember a boyhood full of warmth and love. One of my strongest memories was of those freezing cold winter mornings. All we had to heat our house was a wood stove and at night, as the fire died down and the chill set in, I would bury myself deeper and deeper under the covers. When I woke up, I would sometimes see little piles of snow that blew in through the cracks of the walls and collected at various places on my bed.

But it was nice and warm under the covers—and I just stayed there buried under the blankets as I listened to my father building the fire in the kitchen. Then my mother would start cooking breakfast and I could smell the bacon or sausage and eggs frying. It smelled so good. In one brave leap I'd jump out of bed and bounce from that cold room to the warm kitchen.

So I can remember a lot of good things, even being as poor as we were. It was not all bad because I had parents who really cared.

What my father in particular cared about more than anything else was that I go to school and get a good education. Not just go to school, but graduate from high school, which none of my older siblings had been able to do. And not just graduate from high school but make even more family history by being the first one to go to college to become a teacher.

I can't tell you how important it was to have someone like my father really believe in me. In doing so, my Dad taught me to believe in myself. And almost from the day I could remember anything, I remembered how he just believed that I would go to college. He talked to me about it a lot. He just assumed I would go to college. I grew up assuming I would go to college—but I never thought much about how to pay for it.

My good fortune, which you can't measure in dollars and cents, continued when I went to school. I was very lucky to have some great teachers. Two who had such a big influence on me were Irvin Carter, the principal, and Gladys King, my English teacher. Whether they recognized something in me or felt sorry for me—or a little of both—I'm not sure. They gave me a lot of encouragement, always saying I could do whatever I wanted to do and be what I wanted to be. I didn't realize at that time that this wasn't necessarily the role of teacher. As I got older and entered teaching myself, I realized how much they had done for me that was over and above teachers' typical responsibilities to their students.

I also realized how fortunate I was to start school in Tupelo in the first grade and graduate there as a senior in a class of just eighteen students. Educators like Mr. Carter and Mrs. King watched and helped me grow up.

They were able to give me a great deal of personal attention and encouragement. Even students much better off than me in the big cities couldn't have hoped to receive the level of personal attention that I did—not then and certainly not now.

That says a lot about small town America. For all of the disadvantages, the lack of wealth, and often-scarce opportunities, there are redeeming values you have a hard time finding anywhere else. It's like that day I told you about at our company headquarters—when we had ninety people working through the night without complaint to process a record day of business so that our sales associates could get paid. I've been in other places where you'd better not be standing in the door at 5 o'clock because you could get trampled to death!

Some people would do anything to escape the kind of childhood I had, anything to try to erase from their minds forever the memories of all the struggling and doing without. I can understand their reaction. But for Shirley and me, ours has been a struggle to stay attached to our roots. While our oldest son, Allen, was young, we had traveled around a lot and then were living in Springfield, Missouri—yet all we could think about was how to get back to the Ada area. Why? So that Allen and later Brent could experience the good things about rural life that we did and attend that little school in Tupelo.

I'm very proud that both of our sons did go to the same school I did, graduating in classes not much bigger than mine. I think they appreciated it, too—even if they did have to listen to their old man give the commencement addresses!

Today Shirley and I live in a rather modest house in the country between Tupelo and Centralhoma—not far from where we both grew up. Our sons and their families live right down the road. Both are in business themselves, being involved with companies that supply ice to restaurants, retail establishments, and other facilities. Both have formed and built their own companies. Both are successful. Neither one has an 8:00 A.M. to 4:00 P.M. job. After all, they are their own bosses.

Allen and his wife, Karen, have blessed us with two wonderful grandsons, Greg and Zane. Brent and his wife, Tina, have a beautiful little girl named Nichole Ann, of whom we are very proud.

A while back I wanted to build a more lavish house, but Shirley said, "Never mind." She reminded me that we're not the kind of folks who care about using our lifestyle as a showcase. "Harland and I haven't really changed much at all through all the years, even after enjoying some success," she says. And she's right.

In fact, Shirley has allowed herself only one very visible luxury since Pre-Paid has made a good deal of money. It's a banana-yellow Mercedes sports car that I knew had caught her fancy. So a couple of Christmases ago, my sons and I decided to surprise her with that car. We had to go all the way over to Springfield to find it and then drive it back to Ada, where we hid it in the barn. Today Shirley can be seen hopping around town in that little car—and while you might assume it's the only Mercedes coupe in Ada, Oklahoma, it's not. There's one more—but it's white!

My First Big Sale

I grew up with a lot of pride and confidence, thanks to my parents and teachers. I believed that if I worked hard enough and never gave up, I could achieve almost anything. My dad instilled that in me, though I didn't realize it at the time.

By age twelve I was itching to test that theory and put it into practice. I realized that as hard as my parents worked, I had to take some serious steps to lift myself up. For one thing, I was kind of embarrassed not to be able to afford the thirty cents a day for lunch in the school cafeteria.

And then a full-page ad in *The Hunter's Horn* really got my attention. It advertised two hounds at the price of $50 for the pair.

I really wanted those dogs. For as long as I can remember, I have been fascinated by the art of the foxhunt—not for the killing part of it but for the chasing part of it. Taken in the right spirit, it is a great, clean sport and a place to make wonderful friends and have a lot of fun.

But $50 to me back then might just as well have been $5,000.

105

My best friend, Steve Breed, and I decided to form a partnership and hire ourselves out to do chores, bale hay, dig fence-post holes, and build fences. But first I had to ask my father and, frankly, I was worried. I hoped he wouldn't get the wrong idea that my wanting to work meant I thought he was somehow failing to support his family.

In fact, he wasn't worried about that—but about something else. He wanted to make sure that this teenage entry into business, with the development of my own stream of income, would not in any way interfere with my education. No matter how much I might be able to make my hard work pay off, I must not become tempted to leave school. I had to finish high school, go to college, and become the teacher he dreamed I would be.

I assured my father that hiring myself out had nothing to do with wanting to leave school and everything to do with buying a couple of hounds! He wasn't too excited about me buying a pair of hounds, but my desire to earn money was okay with him.

My father was satisfied and gave me permission to proceed. It was my first big sale. Steve and I spent every spare moment (and with school, studying, and our own family chores, there weren't too many of them) taking on every odd job we could find.

Within two months I had saved up $25—enough to strike a deal with Wofford Battles, a neighbor who had two running hounds for sale. Realizing that dream showed me how hard work and determination could pay off, and it was the beginning of a lifelong love affair with the sport of foxhunting. As I said, it is the sport of it, the running, training, and caring for the dogs—and the relaxing opportunity to get away from business and make a whole different group of great friends—that has always appealed to me.

Shirley loves it almost as much as I do. Today we have about sixty hounds and we house most of them in their own air-conditioned kennel on our property. I have to say, those dogs enjoy more in the way of luxuries than either Shirley or I had growing up! We're crazy about all of them, but for me nothing can ever beat the feeling I had as a teenager when I set my sights on what seemed like an impossible dream of buying the first two hounds.

Going to College

Speaking of impossible dreams: These days, going to college is more important than ever, and for most families and students, paying for it can be a tremendous burden. Yet since so many people do it, it just doesn't seem like that big a deal. But, believe me, it was a very big deal back in Tupelo, Oklahoma, in the early 1950s for a couple of sharecroppers and their son. Without Mr. Carter and Mrs. King, it never would have happened. What I'm most grateful for is not what they did for me by paving the way for me to go to college, but what they did for my father. They made my father's biggest dream come true.

As my high school graduation approached, there was simply no way financially I could go to college. There just wasn't any money. But fortunately, I had pretty good grades. So Mr. Carter and Mrs. King went over to East Central Teachers' College (today it's East Central University) in Ada and got me an academic scholarship that paid my tuition.

But there was still the problem of how to live. I would need about $60 a month for room, board, and books.

Even though we lived just twenty-seven miles down the road, I had only been to Ada once. To me, it was the big city. The second time I went there, it was to look for work so I could support myself in college. I came back empty-handed. Again and again over a period of weeks I hitchhiked to Ada to hunt for a job but could find nothing. The prospect of going to college seemed to be slipping away, and my parents and I watched that happen with great frustration.

But Mr. Carter came to the rescue again. He lined up a job for me at Bayless Drug Store in Ada. The seventy-five-year-old Mr. Bayless very kindly put a struggling student to work delivering prescriptions and stocking shelves, and, thanks to Mr. Carter, I was the lucky one who was chosen for the job in the new semester. We didn't have a phone in our house, so Mr. Carter just drove on over with the good news. I can't tell you how grateful my parents were for all he did to help me.

I worked at Bayless Drug Store for four years, all through college, while I studied for a B.A. in education. It was only with that kind of help from the likes of Irvin Carter and Gladys King that I made it. Even in college, Mrs. King on more than one occasion worked with me if I had problems with my studies. She was just happy to do it. Those are the reasons I was able to prevail.

I remember one evening in particular when I went to the home of her and her husband, Floyd, for help on a term paper. She cooked a great supper. After dinner she helped me with the term paper. Then she and Floyd encouraged me to complete college.

Moving from Tupelo, where my class had all of eighteen students in it, to the "big city" of Ada, where I attended a college with five hundred other students in my class, was a big shock to me. Soon after I got there, I had to start stretching my dollars. Three of my classmates and I did that by leaving the dorm and sharing a small two-room apartment, splitting the $35-per-month rent four ways.

I also quickly set about the business of becoming a teacher. The first order of business was improving my ability to communicate and, more important, finding the confidence to stand up in front of groups of people to talk. That idea scared me to death. So I took speech and debating classes to overcome my fear and shyness and to learn public communications. I would later find out that these skills are essential in almost every field—especially teaching and even more so in sales and business.

Shirley

I didn't know it then, but as I was starting college over in Ada, Marvin and Sallie Thompson had finally managed to move their family back to Lula, Oklahoma—the small town seven miles up the road from Tupelo that they considered home.

For years, the Thompsons made a living the best way they knew how—following the crops from farm to farm from Western Oklahoma all the way out to Arizona and California. Now that they were back in Lula, their teenage daughter Shirley prayed they would be able to more or less settle down. She wanted to stay in the same school for more than just a few months, to make friends and grow up with them.

But there were only a few students in the school in Lula, so it was closed and Shirley found herself being bused those seven miles to the school in Tupelo. At least it wasn't a thousand miles away in some strange place, in a school where all the kids would never see each other again after their itinerant farmer families all went their separate ways.

It's kind of interesting to look back on your life and think about the events and decisions that looked small or inconsequential at the time but that turned out later to have changed your entire life. For Shirley and me, Lula closing its school was one such event because it put her in the school I had attended. Another was the sudden urge I had after a year of college in the "big city" to visit the school and see my old friends and teachers.

Little did I know that would be such an important decision. But it was, for it led me to the most important person in my life for all of my life. As Steve Breed and I drove up to the school and got out of the car, that beautiful sixteen-year-old girl was looking out of the window along with a couple of girlfriends and checking us boys out.

Hard as it is for me to figure, Shirley thought I was "cute" and as soon as she confided as much to her girlfriends, they nudged her out the door to meet me.

It may be corny, it may be a cliché, but it was love at first sight. Shirley grew up much the same as I did. We understood what the other had been through. In a way, she had it even tougher because her family had to move around so much. But even back in Lula, the grueling work never went away. Every day after school, the bus would pick Shirley and her classmates up, but instead of dropping her off at home to study or play, she was dropped off at the edge of the fields to fill bags of cotton.

As close as we are, there are some things about our growing up that we just don't talk about—not even to each other. Those memories are just too painful or embarrassing. But we know and we understand. Our roots are the same—more important, so are our dreams. After forty-one years of marriage, our love is deeper and we are closer than ever. Shirley and I have always done everything as a team and whether the subject is family or business or life, there is no one's opinion I respect or listen to more. From my earliest days as a teacher when I went on the road to coach the student debate team, to my trips to Wall Street and to company meetings around the country as a corporate CEO, Shirley almost always traveled with me. Neither of us would have it any other way.

Of course, my first order of business after meeting Shirley was to convince her parents that they should let their sixteen-year-old daughter date this college man from Ada. I made the sale! It wasn't too long before we were both going to our parents—me at age twenty and Shirley at eighteen—to say that we wanted to get married.

> Shirley and I have always done everything as a team and whether the subject is family or business or life, there is no one's opinion I respect or listen to more.

My father's only concern was the same one he had had eight years earlier when I told him I wanted to go to work. I had to finish school, in this case, college, no matter what. No matter how great the pressures might be to support a wife, and perhaps soon after, a young family, nothing should take my eye off that goal.

I assured Dad that our plan was to have Shirley move to Ada with me and get a job to help make ends meet. And that's what we did. We were married on August 22, 1958, and shortly thereafter, Shirley, for the first time in her life, moved to the city. She got a job at Gwin's Drug Store right across the street from the Bayless Drug Store where I worked. Despite the heartbreak of having

Shirley's first pregnancy end in a miscarriage (and there would be more before we were blessed with Allen in 1963 and Brent in 1971), we were very happy and filled with anticipation about the future.

There were a couple of times I wanted to quit college, particularly when I was offered what sounded like a great job with a pharmaceutical company. Shirley said, "No!" and I didn't quit. Several times in my life she has said, "You can't quit!"

Teaching

All I could think about on graduation day was what it meant to my parents, especially Dad. He had dreamed of this day for so long and now it had come true for his youngest son.

His dream that I become a teacher would soon come true as well. A couple of months after graduation day, Shirley and I U-Hauled all of our worldly possessions to the town of Chandler, Oklahoma, where I was hired to teach high school English and coach the speech and debate team. Two years later, we moved on to Okmulgee High, fifty miles east.

I taught school for a total of six years and for the first few, I thought it would be all I ever wanted to do. Teaching may not seem like such a prestigious job today, which is kind of sad, but it was a very big deal to my family and me. Being able to tell their friends and acquaintances that their son Harland was a teacher made my parents burst with pride.

As a teacher I worked incredible hours. Preparing lessons, teaching my classes, grading the papers, coaching speech and debate, directing school plays, and creating winning debate teams and taking them on the road to competitions filled every waking hour of virtually every day.

The hard work didn't bother me at all. But I came to realize that I was making the same amount of money as the teachers down the hall who taught their classes and went home. And it didn't really matter how hard I worked or how good I was, I just wasn't going to make a whole lot of money. I was willing to put in the time, but I was not in a position to profit from it. This began to trouble me, but I didn't know what to do about it. I would soon find out.

Burning Bridges

In 1966, a good friend and former teaching colleague named Charlie Walls walked into my room at the end of classes and made me an offer I couldn't refuse.

Charlie had left teaching to sell insurance for the National Foundation Life Company. Chairman and CEO Nick Pope had just implemented a "Get-A-Man Program," in which each of his top salespeople was supposed to recruit another salesperson. Charlie was out to get me!

I had a great deal of respect for Charlie. He was a teacher, an ordained preacher, and a cattle rancher as well as an insurance salesman. I was impressed by what he was accomplishing financially for his wife, LaVerne, and family. He was earning enough money to buy one hundred head of cattle and the land to graze them on. As I was the son of sharecroppers, that got my attention. The big shiny tank of an Oldsmobile Charlie drove made a strong impression, too!

I enjoyed teaching and found working with the kids very rewarding. But as I said, I had to consider what a future in teaching would mean to my own family. Didn't Shirley and Allen deserve a life that was more than just hand to mouth? I wanted to set new goals for myself, and the prospect of building a network of customers and working in an industry where we were rewarded for our hard work and success strongly appealed to me. In commission sales, there would be no such thing as that "teacher down the hall" who worked half as much as I did and got paid the same money.

I decided to go for it—but when I went to see the school superintendent to hand in my resignation, I was immediately confronted with another decision.

"Harland," he said, "I'll tell you what. It's June now. School's almost out for the summer. Why don't you go try this insurance thing and I'll hold your job open for you as long as I can. If it doesn't work out, you can come back."

It was one of the nicest offers I had ever received. This was an offer I just had to refuse!

I believed then, and I feel even more strongly about it now, that sometimes in life you have to burn your bridges. If I knew I could retreat to the comfort of that teaching position, chances were I would fail in insurance. In some inexplicable, incalculable way, my determination to succeed would not be as great as it would be by putting everything on the line.

Burning bridges takes a lot of courage, especially when your family's livelihood and not just your own is at stake. I'm not suggesting that people make impulsive or reckless decisions about their career and finances. But sometimes there comes a point when you've done all the worrying and studying and second-guessing and you just have to be bold. You have to grab for that brass ring and not look back. Burning your bridges can give you that extra motivation you need to win. Because when there's no turning back, there's only one direction left to go— forward!

Still, leaving teaching was tough. I remember Shirley trying to understand how I would actually get paid in the commission sales business and how she would manage our household finances with those erratic payments instead of the small but steady paychecks from teaching. Yet she encouraged me to go for it.

But it was my father who was the most concerned and disappointed. He was so proud that his son had become a teacher and he worried that I was throwing away a tremendous accomplishment. I could see him and my mother sitting there, wondering what they would tell people about their son now that he was no longer a teacher.

Nonetheless, in June 1966 I marched into a new world. I'd like to tell you that as a salesman I was a smash from the start, but I wasn't. In fact, I was really worried—worried that I'd mess up my presentations and that I wouldn't be slick enough or tough enough to close any deals. But all those worries just pushed me forward harder. Fortunately, I had burned all my bridges behind me.

Just like at Tupelo High, I was once again blessed with great teachers in Charlie Walls, John

> Sometimes there comes a point when you've done all the worrying and studying and second-guessing and you just have to be bold.

Salter, and Nick Pope. They were great people, as is Laverne Walls, who became especially close friends with Shirley. It was ironic—no sooner had I left teaching than I learned all over again how essential education and training are to success in any field.

The most important thing my new teachers taught me was to do this job with passion and confidence and to always try to find a connection between yourself and the person you were selling to. These things are a hundred times more important than having a lot of expertise or being super slick and smooth. The biggest sale any salesperson makes is when he sells himself. You must believe in what you sell. And you have to relate the value of the product to the person you are trying to sell it to. If you do that and you work hard and visit enough folks, the passion will come through and you will succeed.

One more thing: Never let the rejections get you down because no matter how good you are, you'll be rejected a lot. That's just the way the world of sales happens to be. You don't have to like rejection; who does? But if you fear rejection, you will not succeed. You can't take the no's personally. People aren't saying no to you, just to your product or the timing.

I'm glad I learned that lesson, because my sales career began with quite a few rejections. But soon, things began to click. Within two months, I was beating all the quotas National Foundation Life had set for me. While I would soon leave that organization due to my lack of confidence in some of my superiors, there was no question I had found a new calling. It would provide me and my family with a lifestyle and a cushion of financial comfort that I never could have found in teaching. Charlie Walls and Nick Pope had changed my life.

After a less than satisfying year in real estate sales in Springfield, Missouri, I had a chance to reunite with Charlie Walls back in Oklahoma, this time for a great outfit called Paramount Life, based in Little Rock. With the entire state as my territory, I not only got a chance to perfect my own sales technique but I learned how to build, train, and motivate an entire sales organization. It was an incredibly rewarding experience to not only make life better for my family but to help others do the same for theirs.

Everything was rolling along just fine until that early Friday morning in July 1969 when I had that head-on collision with a new destiny!

Chapter 6

AGAINST THE ODDS

A s soon as I could move around after my accident, I drove over to see a local Ada lawyer. I was still really hurting. I had a brace on my back for my injured spine and compressed discs, and what's more, I felt like my wallet had been surgically removed by this crazy litigation that could cost me thousands of dollars for an accident that wasn't my fault.

But I was numb to the pain that day because what I really wanted to talk to the lawyer about was an idea I had that had been triggered by my problems stemming from that crash. Once that idea invaded my brain, there was no getting rid of it. I couldn't push it to the side, smother it with doubts, or kill it with practicality.

I wondered why there was no pre-paid legal protection plan readily available for an average guy like me who suddenly and unexpectedly found himself and his family on the brink of ruin because of a legal action against him. After all, pre-paid medical protection had been available in America for some thirty years. Over in Europe, pre-paid legal plans had been around for years and were widely used and accepted. As far as I could tell, the only thing that came close to the concept in our country were the small groups of lawyers fresh out of school who, to get their new practices off the ground, banded together to offer a specific set of services at lower than normal prices—a kind of "buyer's club" for lawyers and their clients.

When I look back now, I think I must have been crazy, dumb, or a little of both to believe that I could actually turn the idea of pre-paid legal services into a national movement and a money-making business. Good ideas are important, but there are thousands, probably millions, of people sitting around having good ideas all day long. Sometimes we call it daydreaming! What's much rarer is being able to act on those ideas—to excite others about them, to get the needed financial support, to keep going in the face of rejection, and to fight on, no matter how long the odds are for success.

Still, how crazy—or dumb—was it to think that I, Harland Stonecipher, living in Ada, Oklahoma, with a family to support, my personal finances drained by expenses from the accident, and no real executive track record to speak of, could start a new industry, spread it across the nation, and change the legal system that had been in operation for some two hundred years?

Today I'm more amazed than anyone that we made it. I can't imagine anyone more unprepared to start, run, and build a successful company. They say that ignorance is bliss and in my case that was true. I had no idea what the problems were when we began and no clue about the array of forces that would line up against us. To be honest, if I'd known how tough it would be, I'm not sure I would have gone through with it!

So I'm glad no one ever told me to my face how crazy and dumb I was. Well, no one except a few bankers!

When I reminisce with Shirley about all the problems and reversals we experienced while trying to plant the seeds for Pre-Paid Legal and then to make them grow, she always reminds me: "Harland, having setbacks is the way we grew up. We're experienced at them. We're good at them. And the hardships we faced with Pre-Paid are nothing compared to the ones we faced *before* Pre-Paid. Of course, you'd do it all again!"

When I look back now, I think I must have been crazy, dumb, or a little of both to believe that I could actually turn the idea of pre-paid legal services into a national movement and a money-making business.

She's probably right—as usual. But when I tell you how much resistance we had to put up with to get my dumb idea off the mental drawing board in my crazy head and turn it into the company we have today, you might see my point as well!

I noticed one thing about the pre-paid legal concept right from the very start. The average people I talked to, almost every single one of them—the lawyers, the small businesspeople, the everyday families and consumers—loved the idea. It made so much sense to them and they grasped its value immediately.

I'll never forget the first informational meeting we had in Ada to present the concept to potential investors, customers, and salespeople. We weren't even in a position to sell any products yet, but folks were champing at the bit. Seventy-three people showed up. One farmer who had driven a considerable distance asked simply, "All right, when do we get to buy it . . . and when do we get to sell it?" Another announced, "This will be the biggest thing to hit Ada since some outlaws took over the town in 1900 and got themselves lynched!"

A few local lawyers helped me put the meat on what was admittedly a bare-bones idea. We focused first on auto-related situations, figuring out a way to offer motorists emergency legal protection and bonding service, as well as cover their attorney costs in traffic court and criminal court. Several years later, we expanded the concept to a national legal service that would cover all kinds of situations and offer unlimited attorney consultation. We expanded and perfected the products just as fast as the regulations and our financing allowed.

The more we talked to people, the more they got excited about it. The value of pre-paid legal protection is so clear and compelling that the one thing we have never lacked in nearly three decades of presenting it is ready customers. Give us a chance to put this idea in front of Middle America and people jump at it.

In fact, a couple of times we had so many customers coming in the door that we had to stop writing business for awhile or we would have gone bankrupt! That happened, for example, in 1987. Because of the cost of commissions on all the new members, and the fees we paid to attorneys, we developed a critical cash-flow problem.

The charitable way to look at how we got ourselves into this situation is that we were a victim of our own success! Between 1987 and 1991 we lost millions because we were so successful in attracting customers. Fortunately, even without writing new business, our existing book of business was so strong that membership fees eventually caught up with and then overtook the expenses. By 1991 we fixed our cash-flow problems, paid off our debt, and substantially increased our overall capacity to handle new business. We then opened the floodgates again and the flood has been pouring in ever since. This time we can handle all of it and more!

So from the earliest days of Pre-Paid to the present day, we have never lacked for enthusiastic customers.

I wish I could say the same thing about bankers, regulators, and the legal establishment. The bankers didn't see how we could make any money, especially in the hands of an untested insurance salesman from Ada.

The regulators were just plain confused. They didn't know what to make of our product. It seemed like insurance to them, but then it wasn't really insurance. It involved providing legal counsel, albeit indirectly, but then we weren't a law firm. Who should regulate us and how? So confused were they that we even had to convince them over a several-year period to let us call ourselves by the name we felt best fit our products—Pre-Paid Legal Services!

Finally, the legal community—particularly the bar associations—thought it would threaten their business and worried that our "bargain basement" legal advice would taint the whole profession.

The enthusiasm among the public, on the one hand, and the reticence and suspicion from all the experts, on the other hand, tells us something important about conventional wisdom versus common sense. I'll take an ounce of the latter over a pound of the former any day.

Capital—The 600-Pound Gorilla on Your Doorstep

The biggest problem was the banks. I know some helpful bankers, but most of them are in business to lend money to people who don't really need it. All the ones I went to with my idea just turned me down flat. So did the institutional investors. I can't say that I totally blame them. Pre-paid legal protection was a new and completely untested concept in America. One local banker made me a $300 loan secured by Shirley's furniture. I needed that money to make payroll.

It was not until we gained some serious traction that the investment establishment wanted to lend us money. Today, the banks would just love to lend us money. Of course, now we don't need it. We have no long-term debt at Pre-Paid Legal and enough cash in our accounts to keep our customer-gathering process cranked up high. I never want to have to put the brakes on that again!

With no support from traditional sources, how did we raise the money to build Pre-Paid Legal and keep it going? I went to the same people who so clearly understood the compelling need for our product—average people, friends of ours, friends of friends, anyone we could pitch and convince to buy shares in our venture. We had to put this machine together with spit and rubber bands and sell it to folks on sheer enthusiasm.

> We had to put this machine together with spit and rubber bands and sell it to folks on sheer enthusiasm.

I could never have done it alone and I didn't. Shirley put in almost as many hours as I did. She's taken down names at our early sales meetings and gone to the drugstore or the five and dime to buy small gifts of appreciation we could present to our top salespeople. Even more important were her suggestions, her moral support, and all the hours she listened to my worries about the latest setbacks and helped me through them.

I don't think Pre-Paid would have made it without a man like Rick Haney. Rick was the best salesman I have ever known. He could talk a dog off a meat wagon, as they say over in Arkansas. But more important, I never met a man who was more optimistic, more confident, and more passionate about what he was doing than Rick. He believed in the Pre-Paid mission as much as Shirley or me. On many a dark day when we were inches from disaster, Rick would boost our spirits with his infectious optimism. His tragic and untimely death from a massive heart attack at age forty-two left a gaping hole in our company and in our hearts that will never be totally filled.

Rick helped us to see that we were able to attract as supporters, and in many cases investors, people who shared my vision and who believed that it was only a matter of time before our company really took off. John Hail was one of them. John was a pastor's son from West Virginia who grew up as poor and as hopeful as I had. Through hard work, brashness, and sheer determination, he scaled great heights in business, becoming a gas station owner in Ohio and moving from there into the furniture business. He sold life insurance in Oklahoma and eventually became president of the company that first wooed me away from teaching—National Foundation Life. Later, he would make millions from investments in real estate, energy, and sports. His subsequent financial reversals in those fields, as you'll see in the next chapter, led him and me to multilevel or network marketing.

From his perch as president of National Foundation Life, John had kept a close watch on us. He knew Rick Haney and how much talent and energy he had. John's motivational skills were legendary and I first met him right before he was to make a presentation to our sales force in Oklahoma City. After we met, John immediately bought some stock. He would later rescue us from impending disaster by providing financial support on more than one occasion.

I think you're getting the picture. Financing has always been the toughest issue for us—just as it is for so many other new businesses. From our first days in business in the early 1970s until as late as the early 1990s, raising enough capital was a constant battle. There's no question that the lack of financing significantly slowed the speed at which we could grow. At other times, it threatened our very existence.

Anyone thinking about starting a business ought to reflect on our experience very carefully. Lack of adequate capital is the number one reason why new small business start-ups fail in our country. You must have a clear picture of how much you need to get started and who will invest it or lend it to you. You need a capital cushion that keeps you going when downturns or unexpected expenses occur. You need money to invest in your own growth or else you'll just spin your wheels until you run out of gas.

Needing money for a new business and getting money for a new business are two different things. You almost have to prove you don't need it to get it.

Lack of sufficient financing can kill you even when you have a great product, dedicated partners and employees, and plenty of customers. It's the 600-pound gorilla hanging out on the doorstep of almost every entrepreneur. It's what wakes you up in the middle of the night.

Many nights I haven't slept at all. Many nights I got up and walked around the yard, trying to think my way out. I read most of the self-help books. They directed me to the Bible. I got my best help here.

As you'll see in the next chapter—when I talk about Pre-Paid's embrace of network marketing—one reason I now favor that business approach is because it solves a critical problem facing American entrepreneurs. It addresses the need for start-up and operating capital by essentially removing the need for it. It costs almost nothing to get in and next to nothing to build a sizable business. Network marketing can help fix entrepreneurship in our country just like pre-paid legal plans can help fix the justice system. Having gone through the precarious, hand-to-mouth existence of an entrepreneur, I want to contribute to *that* fix, too.

I'm from the Government . . . and I'm Here to Help

Today governments are tripping all over themselves trying to figure out how to regulate the commerce, companies, content, and technologies that make up the Internet revolution. But the concepts are so new that the old regulatory approaches just don't fit.

The same was true for us back in the early 1970s. When we wanted to open for business in Oklahoma under the name Sportsmen's Motor Club, state officials didn't know what to make of us. They basically told me, "It looks, sounds, and smells like insurance so we think we ought to regulate you. But we don't really know how because we don't know what type of insurance it is."

That was a big problem. Today, we know exactly what's expected of us in every one of the fifty states. In some states we're considered to be a form of insurance, so we're regulated as such. In other states the reins are looser. Sometimes we have to modify certain elements of our products from state to state. We take a very hands-on approach, seeking up-front decisions from each state and regulatory agency. And we work hard to develop healthy working relationships with regulators.

It's no easy task to sort out all of these different requirements. We deal with insurance departments, state attorneys general, consumer affairs departments, and state bar associations (which in many states have government-like powers). If the people who buy and sell our products knew about the extent of our efforts to remain in good standing with hundreds of different state laws and thousands of regulators, they'd be even more impressed by the low cost of the products and business opportunity we offer.

But in the beginning, it was kind of tough when government people—who with a single edict could decide whether our business lived or died—said we ought to be regulated but they didn't know how to do it.

Faced with that situation, the government did what governments usually do when no clear course of action emerges—nothing. Government officials sat on their hands and we were left with no business. And we couldn't start without their go-ahead!

So we did something pretty unusual for any company. We came up with the first method of regulation ourselves and asked the government to impose it on us. We knew officials wouldn't let us operate until there was some oversight, so we essentially said, "Please regulate us!"

Our research found a possible opening for us in the regulations governing motor clubs. We believed there was clearly a provision in that protocol that would allow us to pay attorneys for auto-related situations on behalf of our members. So that's how we proposed being regulated—as an auto club.

They bought that at first, but almost immediately other problems arose. In order to market the legal services we wanted to offer in motor vehicle accidents and disputes, we put right under the name Sportsmen's Auto Club the descriptive phrase "A Legal Service Auto Club."

No way, state regulators told us. Why not, we asked? The answer was essentially that we couldn't call ourselves that because no such animal exists.

It was a bureaucratic Catch-22. We were trying to pioneer a new industry and create something that hadn't existed in Oklahoma or even America. Because it hadn't existed before, in the eyes of many bureaucrats it couldn't exist.

We weren't allowed to brand ourselves or market ourselves in a way that told customers what we were trying to do for them. We could only use our top-line name—despite the fact that we were covering more kinds of car-related situations and paying out more in attorney fees than auto clubs had ever done before.

> We were trying to pioneer a new industry and create something that hadn't existed in Oklahoma or even America. Because it hadn't existed before, in the eyes of many bureaucrats it couldn't exist.

Not only were we restrained from promoting the core business we wanted to be in, we were forced to enter a business we didn't want to be in. The state insisted that if we were going to operate as a motor club in the legal sense, we had to offer all the services such clubs were supposed to offer. So against our will, we found ourselves in the business of towing, jump-starting, and jimmying open car doors when the owners locked their keys inside!

The authorities offered no better explanation for this edict than to say that's just what motor clubs do. That was their thinking. People have a lot of trouble with change, particularly regulatory bodies. Something new or different just seems to scare many people.

They didn't want us to promote the product in the way we saw the product, and they insisted we offer products we weren't interested in. And remember, we didn't have the best kind of financing to do any of this!

Once we had a meeting with members of the Insurance Department in Oklahoma City and they really chewed on me. They said, "You're attempting to do things outside what the regulations provide—and unless you stop, we will have to issue a cease and desist order." They were really tough on that.

My friend Nick Pope attended that meeting with me. He thought it was funny. He said, "If you are going to be in this business, you'd better learn to like this kind of meeting." I never did, but I now understand what he meant. Nick was my mentor.

Keep in mind, at that time all I was trying to do was to offer legal counsel and defense in the event of auto-related incidents. I thought that was a good place to start the pre-paid legal concept because that's where I had had my trouble. But even that was too much for the government.

In those early years we were constantly threatened with shutdowns and investigations. I was called on the carpet in Oklahoma City more than once. Our marketing materials and techniques were constantly scrutinized and on many occasions, as I have said, the regulators tied our hands behind our backs with rules about what we could and could not say about our products.

Another example: When we got the idea to expand our legal services to unlimited consultations with attorneys (the product that today is known as Title I of our Family Plan), that really left the regulators spinning and sputtering!

At first, the Insurance Department said okay and we began to offer it. Then they came back because of some complaints (probably from the legal community) and said that attorney consultation doesn't fit under the Motor Club Act. They told us: "It cannot be part of your brochure. It cannot be part of your motor club membership. You can't even mail information about the product in the same envelope." So we had to incur the expense of a completely different marketing plan, different brochures, and different mailings just to be able to offer average people a simple but valuable service whereby they could call an attorney anytime they needed one!

I don't believe that the government folks in Oklahoma City were bad people. Some were even quite helpful, trying to work it through with us. It was the natural resistance to change that stood in our way more than anything. We saw the same thing happen years earlier when the franchising revolution hit in America. Congress came very close to outlawing the whole concept! And in 1979, the Federal Trade Commission issued a landmark ruling declaring that Amway, the pioneering multilevel marketing company, was in fact a legal business and not a pyramid. Had the ruling gone the other way, the network marketing industry today would be dead in the water, and millions of entrepreneurs would be denied the only kind of business opportunity they can afford. Today, who knows what the impact will be on the e-commerce revolution by the government's various attempts to tax it and regulate it.

The Bar Tries to Quash Our Notion

If our struggles with the banks and the government were not enough, we also found it very hard to win acceptance from the legal establishment. Even though many lawyers I talked to individually were thrilled by the pre-paid legal concept and believed it would be a boon for business, dealing with the bar associations in Oklahoma and around the country was another matter. I thought I'd never live to see the day when the American Bar Association would publicly embrace pre-paid legal service as an effective and welcome approach to giving average citizens access to justice. But they have and I'm still here!

In order for the pre-paid legal idea to work for the client and be financially viable for our company, we needed cooperation from the legal community in three critical ways:

○ We had to find some way to control our costs. Open-ended expenses with no rules of the game would kill us.

○ We had to do more than just pay for our members' lawyers; we had to help them find lawyers as well. Most people had no idea where to turn.

○ We had to find some way to guarantee the quality of the legal counsel we arranged. Both the outcomes of our members' cases and our business reputation were at stake.

Fall short on just one of these and Pre-Paid Legal would collapse. Yet for a number of years, we grappled with a legal establishment that couldn't—or wouldn't—change and adapt to these realities. Ray Kroc found the same thing when he started McDonald's. People already frying hamburgers weren't willing to change. Doing it differently was what built McDonald's and Pre-Paid Legal.

When we first started to offer our service, we said that we would pay, on behalf of our members, "regular and customary fees" for their lawyers. That was the phrase the state bar association itself used. But around the same time, that accepted practice was struck down by the state Supreme Court. The Court said it amounted to pre-setting prices and therefore violated antitrust laws. So that was our first problem. We were told that we couldn't talk about a regular and customary fee because there is no regular and customary fee.

So we started saying we'd pay a certain number of dollars per half-hour of consultation. People who bought the membership were then invited to choose their own attorney, knowing that our plan would pay up to that amount for their lawyer's time.

On the surface, choosing your own attorney in what is called an open panel arrangement has a lot of appeal, just as choosing your own doctor does. The problem is that most of our members would end up calling us because they didn't know any lawyers. "Would you please give us a name?" they would ask. We started doing that until some lawyers complained that we were playing favorites. Next thing I knew, I was called to a Bar Association Board of Governors meeting in Oklahoma City and they told me I couldn't refer people to lawyers.

Looking back, I'm not sure they had any legal basis for saying that, but they were the provider community I had to rely upon. I needed their cooperation and involvement. They told me, in effect, that we might not be able to control you, but we can control the involvement of our lawyers. We can pass a Bar regulation ordering members not to participate. They had me in a bind. Really helpful, weren't they? Just one of many helpful suggestions. The doctors did the same thing in the early days of pre-paid medical plans.

"So what are my options?" I asked. They said they had a referral system. All we had to do was have our members call in and the Bar would point them in the direction of a lawyer. But there was a big problem with their system. They referred callers to lawyers in alphabetical order. It didn't matter what the subject was or a particular lawyer's area of expertise. There was no quality control whatsoever.

To make matters worse, some of these lawyers didn't want referrals and they just flat out told our customers that they wouldn't speak to them. Some of the attorneys were rude in turning our members away. It was not exactly the kind of helpful service I had envisioned providing!

So the next thing we did was run an ad in the *Bar Journal* to ask which lawyers wanted to participate in pre-paid legal work and would be willing to take referrals at the price we offered.

That was an eye-opening experience for us—and for the legal establishment as well. The lawyers responded in droves! We filled a small room with their replies. Attorneys were looking for business and saw this as a good opportunity. Even lawyers from some of the major firms said they wanted to participate.

Now we knew who wanted referrals and who would take them. But Bar officials then told us we couldn't just pick from those lawyers ourselves. There could be no playing favorites. Their theory was that the certificate an attorney had hanging on his or her wall was all the quality control our members or we needed. I think that's still their theory—and you and I know it's not really true. That's not really quality control. I don't believe they teach quality control or customer service in law school.

And, we still had many problems with customer service. Calls to a law firm from our members normally went to the bottom of the pile. Economics normally dictate the place in the pile or the order in which lawyers get to a case.

What the Bar finally allowed us to do was to go down the list in alphabetical order and give the member three names to choose from. That didn't work very well either, but we did it for some time.

With Pre-Paid Legal, I have always considered myself in the consumer product business, yet for more than a decade, we had little control over the content and quality of our product. We suffered for it and so did our members. We knew this because many of our customers told us. They complained about the fact that they weren't getting called back.

They also spotted many situations in which lawyers overbilled us. When we paid the lawyer, we'd send a copy of the check to the member. Often the member would then call us back really mad and say, "I can't believe you paid the lawyer that much. He didn't do anything!"

We found that while in some cases the service was very good, it was completely a hit-or-miss process. We got more complaints than praise.

Controlling our costs soon became as serious an issue as controlling the quality of the service. When our range of services was small, we were able to cap the fee in a pretty clear fashion. But when we expanded it and began to offer more benefits, including open-ended consultations, the open panel approach of letting people choose their own lawyers at a "reasonable hourly fee" just killed us. We almost went bankrupt.

We had lawyers putting in lots of hours—at least, according to their bill. Some billed us for exorbitant amounts. These lawyers were not the majority but rather a minority—yet the minority was enough to kill you. They were just milking us. Again, we sent copies of the checks to our members and again we got those same incredulous phone calls. "I can't believe you paid that guy for five hours of his time. I didn't talk to him for more than fifteen minutes!"

So we really had no way to question these lawyers' fees or monitor their service. That led us to go back and set caps on almost everything, which only triggered more instability and uncertainty in terms of which lawyers would be willing to participate when our members called.

I was desperate to find another way to provide good service for our members, to help steer them through the complicated legal system and find just the right lawyer for their case. I wanted to be able to realize the economies of scale by pooling our members and their fees together so that we could negotiate great deals with the best law firms in the nation. And without in any way interfering with the attorney–client relationship, I had to find a way to monitor the quality of service these law firms were providing our members.

But more than a decade after starting Pre-Paid Legal, we were allowed to do little or none of this. There was no other choice than for us to try to survive in the only system that was permitted. And the brutal fact was that the American Bar Association would not allow us to offer anything but that open panel approach. They cut us off from doing it any other way.

It wasn't until 1987 that we were permitted to develop a closed panel system where we would select the law firms, refer members to specific lawyers, negotiate a per-member payment to those lawyers, and strictly monitor quality and customer satisfaction. Today the overwhelming majority of the legal service products we sell are closed panel plans and this approach means that finally, at long last, I have quality control over the products I sell to the public. The buck now stops nowhere but with me.

We've come a long way with the legal community. Today, I'd say the pre-paid legal concept is totally accepted and the American Bar Association has gone on record endorsing it.

Our reputation among lawyers has improved markedly as well. In the early days, firms that already had a pretty good clientele were worried about their image with those clients if they got involved with us. They were concerned that it might have a negative impact on their prestige. That attitude has almost totally evaporated. Most lawyers realize this is the wave of the future. I'm particularly proud of the fact that for three years running, the Oklahoma attorney general has been the opening speaker at our national conventions and always has good things to say about the positive impact we're having on the access to justice in America.

The Perils of Going Public

As a public company, trading first on the NASDAQ, then the American Stock Exchange, and now the New York Stock Exchange, the Securities and Exchange Commission also regulates us. That has brought its own set of challenges. In the early stages we had to go back and change our system of accounting, just as Ray Kroc had to when he prepared to take McDonald's public.

And I'll never forget the longest seventy-two hours of my life—the time when the Oklahoma Securities Department decided to launch a full investigation on us before it would allow us to sell any stock. They subpoenaed all the members of our sales force and hauled them before a battery of government lawyers. They didn't find anything wrong.

Another time there was a $100,000 block of stock overhanging the market. If it was dumped, this could have finished us off. It would have driven our collateral used for our lenders down to nothing.

I went to see John Hail. I hated to do it. A couple of years earlier when we had one of our cash-flow crises, John and the National Foundation Life agreed to buy a 25 percent block of our stock. For some time after that, I had to drive ninety miles from Ada to John's office in

Oklahoma City and present him with that day's sales contracts. He'd cut me a check so I could go back to Ada and pay the commissions. Those were tough days. One time I realized I didn't have enough gas in my car to get home and not enough in my wallet to fill the tank. John fished a $10 bill out of his wallet and gave it to me.

Now, here I was again with a new crisis and, without batting an eye, John said he would personally put up $100,000 to buy that stock, if and when it got dumped on the market.

Having your stock traded publicly also means you're always at the mercy of broader market trends and the constant scrutiny and prognostications of the analysts. We've seen our stock price driven down to pennies on the dollar by short sellers and by the sometimes-destructive self-fulfilling prophecies of the Wall Street experts. All it takes for a major disruption in your financial picture is for some analyst to circulate a negative opinion about your business fundamentals or the future of your stock price. His opinion is then picked up and repeated by others. The impression spreads through the market and investors start selling. The price goes down and the analyst who made the original prediction looks like a genius!

Remembering What's Important

From the moment we opened our doors in 1971 as the Sportsmen's Motor Club right up to the early 1990s when we were still digging our way out of debt, any number of things going the wrong way could have put us flat out of business. Like I said, it's a miracle we survived. But no matter how tough it got, we never gave up. Our entire team, some of whom have been with us since the very beginning, believed so strongly in the mission of equal justice under law that surrender was just not an option. We were pioneering a new industry and we were the most unlikely people to do it. But no matter what problems we had with money, with the government, with the legal community, or with the markets, I really believed there was just no stopping an idea whose time had come.

The average people we were trying to help believed in it. If only there were a way to put that idea in front of more people, faster and better all over the nation, there would be no stopping us. Pre-Paid Legal could finally reach a plateau where we could really get on with the business of changing America for the better and not just worry about how to pay today's commissions and bills. While it would not put an end to all our challenges, in 1982 we found a way to do just that.

Chapter 7

THE PRE–PAID LEGAL
BUSINESS OPPORTUNITY

Considering the hurdles we had to overcome in our first ten years of business, I should have been very pleased. Even with all the resistance, the misfires, and the close brushes with bankruptcy, we put Pre-Paid Legal on the map as an up-and-coming company offering a compelling product to a potentially huge market. No truly threatening competitor had yet appeared.

But something was gnawing away at me. The market for our product was huge, but things were moving too slow. We started as a traditional marketing company, paying agents on a commission basis—trading paper for paper, as they say in the insurance industry. Using this approach, we were rolling along okay, building a decent book of business and staying alive. But I knew that just staying alive wouldn't create the kind of change I wanted to bring to the legal system or produce the kind of business success I wanted for all the salespeople, investors, employees, and others who had poured so much of themselves into the Pre-Paid Legal mission.

There had to be a better way to grow our company and get the word out about products that could change people's lives. We just needed to get in front of more people.

We found that better way—and it was to build around our products an attractive business opportunity that offered our sales associates a real stake in American entrepreneurship—an opportunity that would be good for them and would put our company on the fast track to growth.

Today, Pre-Paid Legal is not only opening up the justice system to those who have never had access before. It is not only helping the legal profession rediscover a sense of purpose and idealism. There's something more—and as one who has been an entrepreneur ever since I gave up the security of that small but stable teacher's paycheck many years ago, I really consider this the icing on the cake. We have found a way to do all that while offering a great low-cost business opportunity that has already attracted more than 200,000 active participants. I'd like to tell you about it and also tell you why, for the right kind of person, it's better than any other opportunity out there today.

At one time or another, most of us have dreamed about being our own boss. And no country offers more opportunity for the individual, regardless of background, to take an idea, a service, or a product and, with a lot of hard work and a little good luck, build a successful business around it.

When you think about what is happening in our society and economy today, I think you'll conclude as I have that there has never been a better time to start your own business—and there has never been a greater need for you to consider doing so.

The way I look at it, there are at least three good reasons why you should really question whether it is safe or smart to rely on just one job, one career, and one primary source of income. To put it simply, it's because the economy is changing, America is aging, and the family is in trouble.

Are You on the Right Side of Change?

Let's look first at what's going on in the world of work. As good as things are in our country, the traditional employment economy is crumbling. That's where workers sell their time to a company in exchange for money and sell their experience in exchange for security.

149

If you simply look at the numbers economists love to cite, it's hard to argue with the performance of the American economy. In February 2000 we broke the record for the longest uninterrupted economic expansion in history. Inflation barely exists. Unemployment is at a thirty-year low. Consumer demand and confidence are high. Millions of Main Street Americans who never invested in the stock market before are building sizable personal portfolios.

But that's only part of the story. The global economy we're a part of is totally unpredictable and the individual's role in that economy—even when it is growing rapidly—is at best uncertain.

Consider, for example, the Asian economic crisis that exploded several years ago and from which the region is still trying to recover. Hardly anyone saw it coming. In fact, a year before it hit, all the political and economic "geniuses" of the world had gathered as they usually do at the exclusive World Economic Forum in the Swiss Alps to pontificate about the future. No one predicted the bottom would fall out in Asia!

The global economy keeps changing rapidly and it's unpredictable. Where will you fit in as industries continue to consolidate? What will happen to your job as corporations become empowered to move not just blue-collar jobs but white-collar tasks offshore—thanks to Internet technology? Your CEO might be in merger negotiations right now. What will that mean to you? When is the last time you heard of a merger that led to an *increase* in professional positions in that organization?

The good times may keep rolling on, but they could roll right over you. A recent report in the *Los Angeles Times* concluded, "For many corporations, downsizing has become a strategy that is used in good times and bad. Senior managers, under considerable pressure from stockholders to increase profits, often take the easiest way by cutting employment costs."

All told, the Department of Labor reports that despite sustained economic growth, 3.6 million workers were laid off during the last two-year period for which statistics are available. These workers had held their jobs for three years or longer. An estimated 6 million more who had been with the companies less than three years also lost their jobs.

The situation has grown worse since that report. In October 1998 alone, firms announced planned cutbacks of 91,500 jobs, the most in three years. In the first ten months of 1998 alone, 523,000 jobs were cut, a pace exceeding the previous year's by 200,000.

In the 1980s, the concept of "just-in-time" delivery was popularized in American industry. In this business practice, companies achieve shipping, warehousing, and production efficiencies by ordering raw materials and components only as they are needed and turn them into finished products only as they are ordered. A more efficient transportation system and sophisticated information technology made this commonsense idea possible.

Stanford University management professor Jeffrey Pfeffer sees a parallel in the increasing industry practice of layoffs as a strategy of first resort, calling the result for workers "just-in-time employment."

"There are some companies that wouldn't hold workers one minute more than they're needed," he told the *Times*. "They will hold inventories of goods for a long time, but they don't want to hold inventories of people."

American free enterprise has brought untold prosperity and opportunity to our society and to countries around the world that have copied our system. But that system is undergoing profound change, and Americans who don't want to be "just-in-time employees" are seeking other options and opportunities—and they're out there!

The Aging of America

There's another big reason why so many are seeking extra sources of income and alternative paths to financial security. America is going to be full of old folks before too long. It will be a real struggle for either them to support themselves or for our society as a whole to support them with the dignity they deserve.

Seventy-six million Americans born during the baby boom years of 1946 to 1964 are now turning 50 at the rate of 10,000 a day. Beginning in the year 2011, when the first boomers reach 65, the ranks of America's elderly will explode. In fact, we're already home to 35 million people aged 65 and above, 12.8 percent of the population. By 2030, 70 million Americans will be 65 or older, 20 percent of the population.

At the same time, with overall population growth continuing to decline, the ratio of working-age Americans to retired Americans will fall rapidly. Take Social Security, for example. In 1950 there were 16 workers for every retirement-age Social Security beneficiary in the United States. By 1960 the ratio had narrowed to 5 to 1. Today it is just over 3 to 1. And by the year 2030, it will be 2 to 1. This means, in effect, that every working couple that year will have an extra person to support in addition to that couple's own family!

What will this mean for you and your family? For the young, it means working harder and longer and paying higher taxes to support the growing ranks of retirees. The retirement age for collecting full benefits will go up and more of those benefits will be taxed. For the elderly who are living more years in retirement than ever before, it will be virtually impossible for the traditional pension and health programs to keep up with the kind of lifestyle they want to enjoy. For all of us, it means doing more to guarantee our own health and retirement security.

As a nation, we've got our work cut out for us. By one estimate, 96 percent of all pension plans will pay at most 20 percent of our current salary when we retire.

According to *Success* magazine, a person 35 years old today making $60,000 will need $150,000 a year at age 65 just to maintain his or her current lifestyle. That means this person would have to save $44,000 a year—100 percent of after-tax income—to live at that level in retirement.

Many Americans are taking some steps to prepare. Twenty-five million people participate in 401k plans that collectively have amassed $1 trillion in assets. Thirty-seven percent of U.S. households invest in mutual funds. Yet still, only an estimated 2 percent who reach the age of 65 are financially independent.

As for Social Security, the burdens on the system are growing, yet many Americans are highly dependent on the program's benefits:

For 63 percent of beneficiaries, Social Security provides at least 50 percent of their total income. For 26 percent, it provides 90 percent of total income. For 14 percent, it is the only source of income. But despite this dependency, the average monthly benefit for today's retiree is $663 for those retiring at 62 and $925 for those retiring at 65. The maximum monthly benefit is just over $1,300 per month.

On top of this, the system is threatened with insolvency—even with today's federal budget surpluses—due to aging among the population and gridlock among the politicians. The question facing families is: Are your savings, pension, and small Social Security check going to be enough to enable you to live the kind of life you want in retirement—a retirement that for many people could extend twenty-five years and more? The answer for most is no.

The Troubled American Family

Facing the uncertainties of the economy and the challenges of aging are not the only reasons why many are looking for new and different work and income opportunities. Concern about family life is driving the search, too. More and more parents are deciding that they want to be around to see their kids grow up!

The traditional family is under serious strain:

○ Since 1970, there has been a 548-percent increase in the number of unmarried couples with children under 16 years of age.

○ In 1993, 31 percent of all babies were born to unwed mothers—up dramatically from 10.7 percent in the 1970s. In 1950, it was just 3.9 percent.

○ There are nearly 8 million single-parent households with children at home.

○ A majority of working-age women are now employed outside the home. This has been a good development for most women, but the impact on children of both single-parent households and working-couple households is unmistakable. Denied the close supervision and nurturing of times past, many youths are drawn into or are victims of destructive behavior.

○ Youth crime is on the rise, even as crime rates overall level off. More than 1.5 million young people in America are arrested for crimes each year. Young men under the age of 18 commit 17 percent of all violent crimes.

o Drug use among young people is on the way back up after a hopeful but short-lived dip in the mid-1980s.

Researchers discovered further consequences for children when parents find they must work both harder and longer outside the home. "Parents are right to be concerned about the squeeze on family time," the *Washington Post* concluded in an in-depth report. "Specialists say that children benefit intellectually and socially when the whole family is together—by listening to adult conversation, learning to relate to siblings, and getting a clearer sense of the family's moral values."

Eager to aid the family finances, pursue career aspirations, and raise a family all at once, many women attempt to carry a near-impossible burden. While *Newsweek* found that men are picking up a greater share of child-rearing and household responsibilities, the burden still falls most heavily on women, whether or not they also work outside the home.

Looking for the Right Opportunity

For millions of Americans, the path of entrepreneurship is so attractive because it affords an opportunity to build something on their own, often with their families by their side. Ideas and creativity count. Hard work pays off. They have the right to succeed and the right to fail. They feel in charge of their destiny.

Indeed, the men and women who own and run the small businesses and who are self-employed represent a significant economic and social force that brings much of the creativity, energy, inventions, and new jobs to our country. Consider these developments:

- There are more than 22 million small businesses in the United States today, businesses that collectively employ half of all the workers and create two out of every three new jobs.
- Women own more than 33 percent of these businesses and are starting them at a rate faster than men.
- One out of eleven American workers is self-employed. The 12.1 million who are self-employed exceed the number of Americans who belong to private-sector unions. We hear a great deal about those unions in the news— but not nearly so much about this strong and growing independent workforce.

Thanks to low-cost information technology and communications, small business owners, the self-employed, and even many in the corporate and professional worlds are doing more work out of their homes. Some

19 million Americans now devote at least part of their workweek to "telecommuting." This has become a promising path for many who are trying to meet family responsibilities and avoid long commutes.

Owning a Business: Dream Come True... or a Nightmare?

Starting a small business and being your own boss or seeking a more flexible home-based work schedule from your company or organization—these represent two responses to the growing uncertainty and the deteriorating quality of life found in mainstream employment. They prove to be satisfying accommodations for millions of people. Yet many others find that these supposed solutions create new sets of problems.

In 1996 just over 170,000 new businesses were formally created in the United States. That same year, 72,000 businesses failed. Indeed, most small businesses shut their doors within the first five years of their establishment.

Starting a small business can drain your family's life savings and force you to go deeply into debt—even mortgage your house—to get the necessary financing. You'll likely need that financing if, for example, you want to buy a good franchise in a substantial business; this can cost you from $100,000 to $500,000!

If you have little or no track record, it can be very difficult to get needed bank loans. A recent survey by the Census Bureau found that even with the current low interest rates, nearly 49 percent of small businesspeople said it had become more difficult to get financing than in the past. And, even with what is reputed to be a strong economy, the number of small businesses reporting a growth in sales fell to its lowest level since 1968. This is a dangerous development because smaller enterprises account for just over half of the output of the entire American economy.

To add to the small businessperson's headaches, all levels of government continue to pile on burdensome and often contradictory layers of regulations. Safety inspectors from the federal Occupational Safety and Health Administration (OSHA) have recently put out the word that they will start applying rules designed for big companies—companies that have at their disposal large human resources and safety staffs, not to mention teams of corporate lawyers—to small ventures as well. We've already seen in congressional hearings how the IRS has been targeting smaller businesses and family farms, which don't have the resources to fight back.

Look for payroll tax hikes, new health-care mandates, and additional mandatory increases in the minimum wage to add substantially to the cost of maintaining employees. And should one of those employees become disgruntled or seek to exploit you, he or she can always find an eager trial lawyer to help take you to the cleaners. Just one lawsuit can put a small company out of business.

Thankfully, the United States is home to millions of entrepreneurs who are courageous, stubborn, or both and who continue to fuel the vital small-business engine of our economy.

The Network Marketing Solution

But there is a better way for many Americans. It's called network marketing and it's catching on like wildfire all over the globe. Here's why:

o   It is a home-based business opportunity. There is no store, no lease—just a phone, a fax, and a personal computer. Your commute lasts for as long as it takes you to walk down the hall.

o   There are no employees, payroll, schedules, payroll taxes, workers' compensation claims—no employee headaches.

o   There is a potential for a rapid increase in income and for high income, because when you are freed of all the headaches inherent in the old model, you are able to focus all your attention on customers, sales, and income.

o   And you develop a secure diversified income, a residual income that pays you over and over for the same activity, one in which you get paid for the efforts of others you bring into the business.

o It's user-friendly. You can work the business just a little to make some extra money while keeping your regular job. Or, you can work it hard and make a lot of money.

Consider these statistics from the Direct Selling Association (DSA), the national trade association of direct selling, of which network marketing is a part, as well as from its international counterpart, the World Federation of Direct Selling Associations (WFDSA).

o There are 9.3 million salespeople in the United States, with 1997 sales of $22.2 billion. In 1993 there were 5.7 million U.S. salespeople, who sold $15 billion worth of products and services.

o Approximately 79 percent of direct-selling firms compensate distributors according to a multilevel compensation structure. These firms account for 80 percent of the distributors and 72 percent of the sales dollars. The remaining firms operate under a single-level compensation structure.

o About 55 percent of direct sellers are women, 26 percent are men, and 18 percent operate as two-person teams.

o Eighty-one percent devote 30 hours or less per week to their businesses, 8 percent spend between 30 and 39 hours, and 11 percent spend 40 hours per week or more.

- Globally, the WFDSA reports that 30.9 million people engage in direct selling, up from 8.48 million in 1988. Some estimates peg the number of salespeople at closer to 36 million, since the WFDSA statistics do not include China.
- Worldwide sales in 1997 totaled $80.5 billion, compared to just $33.3 billion in 1988.

Pre-Paid Legal and Network Marketing

Now let me guess what some of you not already in our business are thinking right about now. You're thinking, "Oh no, don't tell me Pre-Paid Legal is one of those multilevel marketing deals!"

I'd like to let you in on a little secret. No matter how many doubts you may have about multilevel, or what is now better known as network, marketing, they don't come anywhere near the kind of doubts I had back in 1982 when just a few days before Christmas, John Hail called and said, "I'm coming to Ada. Let's get together over at the Holiday Inn. There's an idea that I want to discuss with you."

I've known John for thirty years. During that time, he has honored me with his friendship always and his support more than once. As I told you in the last chapter, he has been there and saved us from the brink of disaster.

John is also the best marketer I've ever seen. So when he told me he had an idea that could finally put us in high gear, I had to listen.

So I did—and if it had been anyone other than John Hail doing the talking, I would have gotten up and walked out!

Things had not been going well for John. The fortune he had worked so hard to build in real estate, sports, and development had fallen victim to industry downturns and business setbacks. The Hails' beautiful mansion was gone—so was the cash and the boat.

It was enough to break the spirit of almost anyone—but not John Hail. In his distress, he reflected on a project he had helped his first wife, Naomi, with—selling diet products for a multilevel marketing company. Even though the company was of suspect quality and its marketing plan unfair to the average distributor, traveling with Naomi to her sales meetings gave John a close-up look at the powerful potential locked inside this business model.

> Thankfully, the United States is home to millions of entrepreneurs who are courageous, stubborn, or both and who continue to fuel the vital small-business engine of our economy.

"I'll tell you who's got the best product for multilevel with the right kind of plan," he told Naomi, "Harland

Stonecipher. I'm absolutely convinced. He's stymied from growing too much until something really revolutionary can turn on their marketing. I've got the revolution!"

As I listened to John in the Holiday Inn coffee shop, it was hard not to think back to that day just two years earlier, when in a moment of crisis I had gone to see John to convince him to buy $100,000 worth of Pre-Paid Legal stock that was overhanging the market. If that stock had dropped on the market during that time when we were so small—and we expected it would—you never would have heard from Pre-Paid again. John was there for me. Besides, $100,000 didn't mean much to him then.

Now here he was two years later with an idea he believed was going to lead to his salvation and mine. But he was asking me to let him do something I really didn't want to do.

"Here's how I feel," I remember telling John. "I am tempted to say that if you think for one minute that I am going to take all the blood, sweat, and tears and flush it with some Mickey Mouse multilevel messing it up, you're crazy!

"But the truth is I've got too much respect for you to believe you'd do anything to mess me up. You've already proved that many times. If you really believe in this, then there must be something to it."

I told John we'd give it a try, but on one condition. He had to pick a place to start that was at least five hundred miles away from Ada. I didn't really want anyone to know!

With that go-ahead, John formed an outfit that he called The Vital Connection, or TVC, Marketing Associates. He quickly devised a compensation plan and a sales campaign for our newest product—this one is called "opportunity."

After just one year, this new marketing approach had doubled our revenues. That got my attention! I began to see its real potential and decided to allow John to make a presentation about it to our full-time sales force—officially granting him a reprieve from the five-hundred-mile rule. There was some skepticism, but one person who was convinced was Wilburn Smith, then our sales force leader and today president of the company. We decided to go for broke and in 1984 began an intensive recruiting effort, with the company's sales force essentially working under John Hail under the auspices of TVC.

The growth and impact I had dreamed about were finally happening! What happened to Pre-Paid Legal during the 1982 to 1986 period when we moved into network marketing spoke volumes to me.

The growth and impact I had dreamed about were finally happening! What happened to Pre-Paid Legal during the 1982 to 1986 period when we moved into network marketing spoke volumes to me. In 1982, we had just $2 million worth of sales revenue. In 1983 it was $4 million. In 1984, $9 million. In 1985, $19 million. And in 1986 we did $42 million worth of business.

As a result of this growth, our stock began to move and the investment community began to take notice. Yet one regularly expressed concern was that virtually all of the company's sales force was owned and operated by someone else—John Hail and TVC. That made some people uncomfortable, people who didn't understand the relationship of total trust and friendship that existed between John and me, and that still exists to this day.

But when the time was right for both of us, John and I made another deal. Pre-Paid Legal acquired TVC and thus owned its own sales operation again. John and his partners acquired Pre-Paid stock.

Doing It Differently

Why did I react with such doubt and suspicion the day John Hail met me at the Ada Holiday Inn to sell me on network marketing? Why do I confront similar doubts and suspicions when I'm explaining our company to the press and to opinion-leaders on Wall Street?

Part of it stems from the sense that network marketing has been a place reserved for those people who have failed at everything else. Unfair as it may seem, I thought we'd run into a lot of ne'er-do-wells in the industry—folks who roam the country from one company to another.

The presence of some dishonest operators also damaged the reputation of the industry as a whole. They built fly-by-night operations with products of poor quality or questionable need and stacked the compensation plan against all but a handful of insider salespeople. They spent more time recruiting than they did on selling product, encouraging participants to spend small fortunes on a variety of tapes, conferences, and training sessions. They overpromised and exaggerated the income results, which is the quickest way to lose credibility and gain legal problems in the network marketing industry.

But the industry has also done a great deal in recent years to enhance its reputation and help the public draw clear lines of distinction between solid companies that are in it for the long haul and those that may be here today but will be gone tomorrow. Today, the solid companies with integrity and good products will survive and help improve the lives of millions of people around the world by giving them a chance they've never had before to own their own businesses.

You won't be surprised to hear me say that I think Pre-Paid Legal is the best of the lot. And even among those companies that are reputable, we do things quite differently.

Some of them still seem to put a greater emphasis on recruiting than on products. Not Pre-Paid Legal. We are a product-driven company, now and forever. One of my cardinal rules is that if a person works hard enough, he or she should always be able to make a substantial income simply by selling the product. Even if you never recruit a single person to sell it along with you, your commissions alone should carry the weight.

In fact, while some companies operate exclusively with network marketing sales forces, Pre-Paid employs a blend of marketing approaches. There are those people who build multilevel organizations. Those who simply sell the product. And there is our critically important group sales division, led by Kathryn Walden, which of late has been responsible for some of our most impressive gains in the marketplace.

The fact of such great gains in the field of employer/employee benefits opens a big recruiting arena. We need more people to call on groups. There are lots of people out there who need new employer/employee benefits to offer to existing clients. What a great recruiting opportunity—all built on a product that meets a real need at an affordable price.

These group salespeople, of whom quite a few make over $100,000 a year, are specially trained to go after employer/employee groups in which a company or an organization has agreed to offer Pre-Paid Legal products as an optional benefit or in some cases a fringe. Our salespeople are then invited in to make the presentation. While some of you may wonder if there is friction between our sales forces, in fact they blend together well. In many cases, network marketing is the feeder system that recruits individuals who then qualify for group sales. Some of our bigger money-earners are networkers who recruit group salespeople.

Many companies are privately held and thus operate in the shadows. Not Pre-Paid Legal. We are publicly traded on the New York Stock Exchange. Anyone who knows anything about the rules and protocols of the Securities and Exchange Commission and the clout of Wall Street analysts knows that this opens every aspect of our company up to intense scrutiny. It's all there for anyone—an investor, an associate, a member, or a reporter—to see and examine. There are few if any secrets when you are a public company.

Some companies go in for showy displays of wealth, and they promote and celebrate their leaders like rock stars.

Not Pre-Paid Legal. We're passionate about what we do, and we believe that the product and the business opportunity we offer are second to none. We believe that mentoring by the most successful associates in our company can be invaluable to those just starting out. And we understand the value of recognition and reward in helping people to move forward.

But we don't have a caste system or foster a cult of personality. We believe that the facts, not the emotions, sell our products. We want to build a business, not another religion. Most of us already have a religion that serves us well and we, it.

I'm not here to criticize anyone else. Each network marketing company has to find its own approach and will acquire its own unique culture. I have a great deal of respect for the industry, especially the pioneers like the Amways and A. L. Williamses, which had to bear the brunt of early ridicule and scrutiny. The approaches they devised and the lessons they learned blazed the trail for the rest of us.

And despite the condescension that remains in the attitudes of many so-called business experts, network marketing today is having a profound impact on the entire business world. The most successful marketing companies in the future will be those that employ a blend of the best features of both network marketing and more traditional marketing approaches.

> Network marketing today is having a profound impact on the entire business world. The most successful marketing companies in the future will be those that employ a blend of the best features of both network marketing and more traditional marketing approaches.

As much as they have disparaged direct selling in the past, consumer product and services companies are realizing that they can no longer afford to ignore the potency of face-to-face (or phone-to-phone and computer-to-computer) selling.

They crave the customer loyalty that is increasingly hard to come by with traditional advertising and marketing approaches. As we've seen, the aging of society is causing an overall shortage of workers. Regulations are driving up the cost of maintaining those workers they do find. Again, these companies look with envy to the successful network marketing companies where a dedicated sales force works with no guarantee of income and no traditional employee overhead.

This system places no limits on what an individual can earn at Pre-Paid. Some earn incomes most people only dream about. A recent study of income in America places those earning in excess of $100,000 per year in the category of being rich. If this is true, we have a lot of sales associates who can consider themselves rich.

With mass media multiplying and with consumers becoming increasingly segmented, how do companies reach them? How do they cut through all the noise? How do they appeal to a public that is spending less and less time watching the major television networks and reading the daily newspapers, while spending more time on the Internet, watching videos, and channel-surfing around 100 to 500 different channels? During those times when the nation does come together, such as on Super Bowl Sunday, how many firms can afford the price of admission to a rarely unified market—$1 million for a single 30-second commercial!

The smart companies have come to understand that network marketing is an important part of the answer. *INC.* magazine has observed, "From the top of *INC.*'s 500 companies to the bottom are product and service companies that have adopted multilevel marketing to control overhead, create means of distribution, and build a national sales force on a budget. All of these companies have tapped into a growing contingent of displaced workers, professionals worried about their future, at-home moms, and couples—all looking to get into business for themselves."

As for network marketing companies, what do they need from the more traditional companies? Answering that question requires some understanding of the environment in which these companies operate today.

- It is a highly competitive environment. With full employment and relative prosperity in the United States, the pool of eager participants in these businesses is limited, and the distributor forces that do sign up turn over continually. That's why I'm particularly proud that our associate sales force is growing much faster than the industry average.
- The regulatory environment is becoming more complex, particularly in the international arena that some companies are counting on for a significant share of their future growth. Despite vast improvements in business ethics, these companies are viewed with suspicion in many countries. In 1998, for example, China overreacted to abuses by fraudulent domestic operators by shutting down the entire direct-selling industry! Other countries require network marketing concerns to invest heavily in local manufacturing and other facilities before allowing them to sell products and recruit distributors.
- The development of unique products and services to be sold through network marketing is becoming increasingly expensive. To be competitive, you need capital. To keep on top of the competition,

you need experienced executive management that understands changing markets. Yes, you even need lawyers to handle all the inevitable liability issues and to keep the class-action-lawsuit vultures at bay. Many of the experts believe—and this time I agree with them—that in the coming years, services rather than hard goods will be products that are most successfully sold through network marketing. Pre-Paid Legal has been a leader in moving the network marketing world into the sector of our economy that is growing the fastest—the service sector.

Few upstart network marketing companies have the resources and the skills to operate in this environment successfully over the long haul. That's why so many come and go—attracting little money, notice, or participation other than from a handful of roving multilevel marketing groupies.

So what do network marketing entrepreneurs gain from joining forces with companies established along more traditional lines? The answer appears to be—the best of both worlds!

In our case, they gain the credibility of a company that is open to full scrutiny and whose stock is publicly traded.

Ours is a company that devised and perfected its products based on a truly compelling need in society and not for the purpose of recruiting network marketers and keeping them busy. For the first ten years, we marketed our product through traditional marketing methods. We proved that people could earn a good living by marketing the product. Wilburn Smith, who is now president of our company, proved that in the 1980s.

Pre-Paid Legal is a company with a solid infrastructure of management, systems, technologies, and quality controls.

Furthermore, as a network marketing associate in Pre-Paid Legal, you don't have all the headaches of dealing with the regulators in fifty different U.S. states and two Canadian provinces. You don't have to worry about what the news media say about us or what the Wall Street investors think about us. You don't have to look over your shoulder for competitors or continually monitor the actions of hundreds of provider attorneys.

You don't get any of those headaches when you join our business. You turn them over to me! All you have to do is go out and see enough people and sell the product—and if you wish, convince others to do the same.

You will be operating like an entrepreneur with a strong and established company backing you up: It's a good place to be—for the associate and the company!

The Pre-Paid Legal Marketing Plan

Okay, but let's turn to the two questions you really want to ask. How do I make money at Pre-Paid Legal? And how much does it cost to get in?

174

You can become a Pre-Paid Legal associate for a one-time fee of $65. That's all it takes to start earning commissions on sales and recruiting other associates into the business so that you can earn money on their sales as well.

However, we strongly recommend that the new associate take advantage of what we call our Fast $tart to $uccess program. It costs $249 and provides you with basic training and the initial forms and supplies you need to get started: computer services that map the growth of your organization; print-outs when you personally write business in a given month; and access to the ongoing training classes that are offered to help you become an effective business manager and sales presenter.

Critics of network marketing often attack company-sponsored training and support. They say it's a gimmick to make money, not a serious effort to educate salespeople.

I find this view curious. I wonder if they criticize the years of costly training it takes to become a doctor or a lawyer or to get an MBA—where students and their families dive deeply into debt with no sure prospect of a high-paying job on the other end. We're a society that highly values education as an enlightening undertaking in its own right, as well as a ticket to opportunity. Why should network marketing be singled out as the only field where good training is *not* important and even wasteful?

Yes, our company will make money from well-trained associates—not from the training itself but from a sales force that is far more effective and successful than it would otherwise be. Most important, the training and support services we offer, as a part of the $249 Fast $tart fee and other programs, will help you get started on the right foot.

Of course, your most valuable resource for learning this business is your upline, the person who brought you in—and that person's wise counsel and comforting words of encouragement won't cost you a cent. Most of these mentors will give freely of their time and advice. It's in their interest to do so, because the more you make, the more they make. That's what's so great about this business model. It replaces an ethic of dog-eat-dog with an ethic of people helping people. The more people you help, the more you help yourself—and the more you earn.

Seeing some early signs of success is important because it dramatically increases the chances that the new associate will stay in the business and see it through. That's why I strongly encourage every new entry not to skimp on a few dollars and to get the training he or she needs to do it right. (As a further incentive to become well-trained, we also start those associates who sign up for the Fast $tart to $uccess at a higher level of compensation for their sales and the sales of their recruits.)

It's also why, despite a great deal of criticism from the financial community, I insist that when our associates enlist a new Pre-Paid Legal member, they receive a three-year advance on commissions from that sale.

I'm able to do that because our legal service products are so compelling that we can be reasonably confident that our members will stick around at least that long. We have an actuarial history over a twenty-seven-year period that bears this out. I want to provide this advance because I've been there myself, trying to make a living on commission sales. I know how discouraging the sales profession can be. And I want to put money in our associates' pockets as fast as we can afford to. That helps them and it helps our company because we have a more dedicated and aggressive sales force as a result.

Making Money with Pre-Paid Legal

So for either $65 or $249, you're in business! When you compare that cost to what it would take to buy into a franchise or open a small retail shop, it's a great deal—even more so when you realize that you have an opportunity to be paid in four different ways:

1. Personal Sales Commissions

   We pay generously and quickly on membership sales, processing the applications and checks you send in within 24 hours of the time we receive them in Ada.

   As I mentioned, we advance three years' commission on the strength of the first month's membership fee, even though the agreement is on a simple, month-to-month basis. For example, as an executive director you can earn up to

$171.87 by selling just one $25 Family Plan to a member!

2. Override Compensation

In addition to personal sales commissions for the business you write, you will also receive overrides on the sales of other associates you bring into our business and on sales of their recruits as well!

3. Residual Compensation

You will also be paid in the future for the work you and your organization do today.

When you and the people in your organization sell memberships, you can receive residual income on those memberships for as long as they stay in effect. The income can be there for you, your family, and generations of heirs.

4. Training Compensation

You can also earn substantial income as your organization becomes trained through the Fast $tart to $uccess program or as you personally follow the Fast $tart to $uccess training programs.

Climbing Pre-Paid's Ladder of Success

While the associate can earn a solid income, as well as strong residual payments in the future, simply on the basis of commissions on membership sales, the real growth opportunity in our business is to build a personal sales organization where you benefit from the collective efforts of others. This is the true economic power of the network marketing approach. I'd like to illustrate step-by-step how we have harnessed that power for the associate's benefit in Pre-Paid. This illustration is based on the scenario of selling a $25 per month ($300 per year) Pre-Paid Legal membership:

Step Number 1 (Level 1)

You become a Level 1 marketing associate by paying a one-time fee of $65. You may sell memberships and recruit other Level 1 associates immediately. You are paid as you earn on your first three marketing sales, $20.83 every year the membership is in force. You are advanced $62.50 on your fourth membership sale.

(Note: if you pay $249 and attend the Fast $tart training class, you can move directly to Step Number 4—Level 4!)

Step Number 2 (Level 2)

Recruit one Level 1 marketing associate and you advance to this level. If you've already made three personal sales, you are now advanced a $70.31 commission on every Pre-Paid membership you personally sell, and you earn $23.43 every year for as long as the membership is in force.

Step Number 3 (Level 3)

Personally recruit two more Level 1 marketing associates or have 25 organizational Pre-Paid memberships and you advance to this level. You are now advanced a $85.93 commission on every membership you personally sell, and you earn $28.64 every year for as long as the membership is in force.

When one of your personally recruited Level 1 or Level 2 associates or anyone in their organizations sells a Pre-Paid membership (and you have made three sales of your own), you are advanced a $15.62 override bonus and earn $5.21 every year for as long as that membership is in force.

Step Number 4 (Level 4)

As soon as you and/or your organization sell 50 memberships, you advance to this level. You are now advanced a $93.74 commission for each one you personally sell, and you earn $31.24 every year as long as it's in force.

When one of your personally recruited Level 1 or Level 2 associates makes a sale, your override bonus now increases to $23.43 and you get $7.81 for every year those sales are in force.

And when one of your personally recruited Level 3 associates or anyone on his or her team sells a membership, you are advanced a $7.81 override and earn $2.60 every year.

Step Number 5 (Manager Level)

As soon as you and/or your entire team sell 100 memberships, you advance to this level. You are now advanced a $117.18 commission on every membership you personally sell and you earn $39.05 every year thereafter.

Now, when one of your personally recruited Level 1 or Level 2 associates or anyone in their organization sells a membership, you get a $46.87 override bonus and earn $15.62 each year.

When one of your own Level 3s sells a membership, you earn a $31.25 bonus and earn $10.41 each year it's in force.

When one of your personally recruited Level 4 associates or anyone on his or her team sells a membership, you are advanced $23.44 and earn $7.81 every year.

Step Number 6 (Director Level)

As soon as one of your personally recruited associates attains the manager level, you will be advanced to the director level. You are advanced a $140.62 commission on every PPL membership you personally sell, and you earn $46.86 every year as long as the membership is in force.

When one of your personally recruited Level 1 or 2 associates or anyone on his or her teams makes a sale, you are advanced $70.31 and earn $23.43 every year the membership is in force.

When your Level 3s make such sales, the advances and yearly earnings are $54.69 and $18.22, respectively.

For your Level 4s, it's $46.88 and $15.62; for your Managers, $23.44 and $7.81.

As your personally recruited associates reach the level of director, they break away and take their teams with them. They become what we call your *1st generation breakaway.* You are advanced a $5.00 override on every sale made by them and earn $1.66 every year that membership is in force.

Your 1st generation breakaway directors will produce your 2nd generation breakaway directors. You get $2.50 on each of their sales and a residual of $0.83.

As your organization grows, this process continues through 12 generations of breakaway directors. On a declining scale, you earn override bonuses and residuals on all of their sales. That can add up to a lot of cash!

Step Number 7 (Executive Level)

The executive represents an extraordinary level of achievement at Pre-Paid Legal. It's really where it's at in our business—and once an associate reaches the executive director plateau, there's another very lucrative ladder to climb from there: from bronze to silver to gold to platinum 1, 2, 3, and 4!

The executive bonus level pays an additional $31.25 advance commission on all sales in the qualifying director's personal team and all his or her breakaway directors' teams—all the way down to the next qualifying executive, regardless of the depth in breakaways. The executive director also earns $10.42 a year as long as the membership is in force. Commissions on personal sales receive bonuses as well.

To qualify, a director must have at least three active first-level directors in his or her organization and at least 75 sales, personal or your organization's director legs. You can also count up to 25 new personal sales to reach the total of 75. But no more than 25 membership sales will count for the qualification from any one director line.

The executive bonus will be on a month-to-month qualification. Qualify one month and receive the bonus the next month. To keep the bonus coming, you will need to continue to build your business and qualify each month from then on. These rewards are very substantial. They are quickly turning our very top performers into millionaires.

Making the Law Work for You

Do all those dollars and cents and decimal points actually add up to something real? Do they offer an individual a hedge against a changing economy? Can they give you and your family financial security and peace of mind as you look toward an enjoyable retirement? Do they allow you to build serious, long-term residual income on a flexible schedule that frees you to spend more time with your spouse and children?

For those who work hard, the Pre-Paid Legal business opportunity gives you the potential to achieve all this and more. You can also be part of a cause greater than yourself—changing the American justice system and helping others build their own independent businesses and financial freedom. You, in turn, profit from their success and your good works.

I've come a long way since the day I wanted to get up and walk out on John Hail when he told me that Pre-Paid Legal should offer associates a network marketing plan. Since that day, my respect for the power and potential of this business model and for most of the people in it has grown enormously.

> You can also be part of a cause greater than yourself—changing the American justice system and helping others build their own independent businesses and financial freedom. You, in turn, profit from their success and your good works.

It is open to everyone, regardless of income, background, or education level.

Its cost of entry is so low that you don't need to take out loans or mortgage your home to participate.

You can work it the way you want to—on the side, while keeping your regular job, or full time, with the prospect of earning some serious money.

You don't have employees. You can run it out of your home. Commute to work by walking down the hall from your bedroom to your den!

Best of the Best—Pre-Paid Legal's Platinum Executive Directors

Bev and Dave Savula,
Platinum 4

Ken and Shirlene Moore,
Platinum 3

Fran Alexander,
Platinum 2

Mark and Denise Brown,
Platinum 2 and Regional
Vice President, Texas

Mike and Michael Dorsey,
Platinum 2

Bake and Millie Baker,
Platinum

Brian Carruthers,
Platinum

Yvetta and Kelvin Collins,
Platinum

Joe and Barbara Dameron,
Platinum and Regional
Vice President,
North Carolina

Toby and Bonnie Cutberth,
Platinum

Jae and Jackie Hoglund,
Platinum

Joe and Ruth Lemire,
Platinum and Regional
Vice President, Ohio

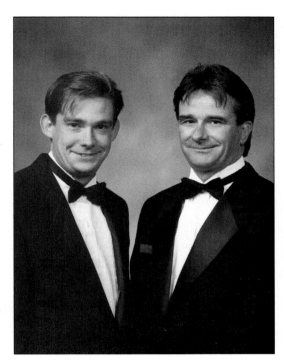

Mike and Steve Melia,
Platinum

Randy and Pat Moore,
Platinum and Regional
Vice President, Oklahoma

Don and Phyllis Whigham,
Platinum

Even though you will be in business *for* yourself, you won't be in business *by* yourself. You'll have a great team backing you up and helping you succeed—from the sponsors who bring you into the business to the dedicated staff in Ada.

And as you will see in the next chapter, you'll get a gift that's precious and rare—the chance to surround yourself with success and gain the support of the entire Pre-Paid Legal family.

By combining the power of a product whose time has come and a business opportunity whose potential for the average citizen is second to none, Pre-Paid Legal can make the law work for you in two significant ways. For a few dollars and a lot of hard work, you can build your own business, be your own boss, strengthen your family, and enhance your retirement. At the same time, you can help others solve their legal problems and protect themselves when they're under legal attack.

It's a win-win for everyone!

Chapter 8

PROFILES OF SUCCESS

Y ou probably know the old conundrum "If a tree falls in the forest and there's no one around to hear it, does it make a sound?" Companies of every type offering all kinds of products and services grapple with their own version of that riddle every day. How do you get the word out about your product in a marketplace that, thanks to the Internet and many other factors, is increasingly segmented and hard to reach? How do you break through all the marketing noise out there and get a chance to appeal to that busy, bombarded, and increasingly skeptical consumer?

You do it the old-fashioned way—face-to-face, one prospect at a time.

I'm convinced that if we can talk to enough people about the low-cost, high-quality legal protection plans we offer, failure would be literally impossible. That's why our associates—the independent entrepreneurs who look customers in the eye and sell our products every day—are the most important people in the world to me. These folks make it all happen. This is why, whenever I talk to them, I call Pre-Paid Legal "your company."

I told you in the last chapter how I came to believe that network marketing is the most powerful distribution method in business today and why it is uniquely suited to selling a product like ours. It has made our business explode and will continue to do so in the years ahead. Now I'd like to tell you about some of the folks who have succeeded at Pre-Paid Legal.

What did it take for them to be successful? How is it that they were able to build their own businesses and earn six-figure incomes and beyond and, at the same time, set their own schedules and spend more quality time with their families—all for an initial investment of several hundred dollars?

Remember that famous scene in the 1968 film *The Graduate,* in which a family friend pulls aside young Dustin Hoffman at a party and confides what he thinks is the one-word secret to success for a young man just starting his career. He whispers: "Plastics." When aspiring Pre-Paid Legal associates ask me what the secret to success is in our company, I say it's "the product."

It's the product. It's that simple. Pre-Paid Legal is a product-driven company. I've learned that you can have the best marketing plan and the greatest information technology, corporate expertise, publicity, and training tools, but if you don't have a compelling product that meets a real need, you won't be around very long.

Our product is strong enough that if an associate does nothing more than go out and sell it—never recruits a single new associate, never builds a network marketing organization—he or she can still make a great living.

There's one other hot tip that I whisper into our associates' ears every chance I get, and that is, "Passion." You have to believe in the product—not just like it, not just think it's a good idea, but really believe that it will help people, even save people from disaster, and help improve our society.

The Biggest Sale

The biggest sale you will ever make is when you sell yourself on the product. That's what sales is all about. The rest is pretty easy. But if you don't make that very first and most important sale—to yourself—you won't make many others. It's true that a salesperson's enthusiasm is infectious, but the lack thereof is even more so. People can sense it a mile away.

At Pre-Paid Legal, getting passionate about the product is pretty easy. I mean no disrespect to other network marketing companies that sell products ranging from soap to vitamins to phone calls. Personally, I'd find it very difficult to get passionate about saving myself and my customers a few pennies on a long-distance phone call or a new kind of laundry powder. Sure, they bring good value to consumers and help independent entrepreneurs build their incomes all over the world. I respect that—a lot—but I just can't get excited about them.

My own background in sales taught me a few things about what's important to success and what is not. When I think about how I came out of a teaching environment into the uncertain world of commission-based sales, I was probably the most ill-prepared, unlikely person to make a success of it. At first, I thought you had to be smooth and glib and have a lot of training. But I soon realized that what you really needed was to believe passionately in your product. If you really believe in it, that will come across. You can stumble over words. Your hands can shake. You can talk too fast or too slow, repeat yourself, and lose your place in your presentation, but if you really believe in the product, that will come across. Your customer will figure that out.

But can I really do this? That's a question we all ask. What does it take to be a success in Pre-Paid Legal? How do I become one of those $100,000-a-year earners who get to join that growing parade of folks who stride across the stage at our annual conventions?

What are the job requirements? What's the right age to be? What about experience and educational background? Does ethnicity, race, or gender play a role?

Let's illustrate the answers to these questions with some real-life examples.

Ten years ago, Kyle Kimbrell was just twenty-three years old. He was working two jobs at the time, earning minimum wage at a store here in Ada and a few extra bucks delivering pizza—all to support his wife and young child.

When his boss at the store found out Kyle was moonlighting, he didn't like it very much. And he told Kyle, "You don't need that extra job anyway. Six more months here and you'll get a 50-cents-an-hour raise."

Now, that's really something to look forward to!

Kyle realized he'd get nowhere fast at that rate, and a second and even a third job wouldn't make much difference. So he decided to start selling Pre-Paid Legal memberships the week before Christmas—just about the worst time you could pick to try to talk to people. But, fortunately, nobody told Kyle that because if someone had, he might not have tried. Just like I might not have tried to start the company in the first place if I knew how hard it would be.

Poor Kyle was so dumb that he tried to sell memberships anyway and, in that one week, made half as much money as he had earned the entire year holding down two jobs. He's still going strong today and ranks among our top ten money earners.

We have a lot of successful associates in their seventies and eighties as well—retirees who wanted to do something useful, fun, and profitable but who wound up making more money in retirement than in the jobs they'd left behind.

As for education, I know Ph.D.s who flopped in our business and high school dropouts who make more than $100,000 a year working for Pre-Paid Legal.

What about race, ethnicity, or country of origin? I think of Jimi Akiboh, a Pre-Paid Legal associate from Indiana. Jimi was born in Nigeria. He may not speak the language here very well, but he is fluent in the language of success. In fact, he likes to tell the story about the time he decided to surprise his wife and kids by buying them a new sport utility vehicle.

"While I was doing that, I decided to surprise me, too. So I bought myself a Mercedes!"

Age, experience, education, health, background—if you're looking for an excuse, you can pick any one of these factors, and I guarantee you it will destroy your motivation!

Spreading the Word

With no roadblocks in your way, what does it take to succeed at Pre-Paid Legal? I come back to the product. Think about how unique it is and you will understand how it can virtually sell itself. You don't have to be that good. You just have to go out and tell people about it.

Suppose that when I sold life and health insurance, I walked into someone's house and he or she told me, "Harland, I'm glad you're here. You see, I'm scheduled to go in next week for open heart surgery." What could I do for that person? Nothing but sympathize and get up and leave!

In our business, what we do would be similar to a health insurance company that goes out and looks for cancer patients to cover. Crazy? Well, maybe. But the fact is, 52 percent of our target market—those 100 million families that comprise Middle America—have some kind of legal problem right now. And for most of the other 48 percent, it's not a question of if, but when.

So if you're an associate or thinking about becoming one, approximately 52 percent of the people you talk to already need you. Except, we don't sympathize and get up and leave. We stay and sign them up. They can sign up on the spot, current legal problem and all, and right then and there call one of our provider attorneys.

How good do you really have to be to sell something like that? I challenge you to fail! If you talk to enough people about Pre-Paid Legal products, you won't fail.

But understand one thing—the phone will not ring by itself with a customer on the other end. You have to make it happen. We like to challenge certain new associates to perform a simple test. For seven days, we ask them to give five presentations a day and fax the results directly back to me. I got one of these faxes recently from a woman who was convinced she couldn't succeed. But she took a chance and rose to the challenge. On her very first day she talked to five prospects and sold three memberships. She faxed me the results and her excitement and confidence jumped right off the page.

What I failed to tell her is that she didn't have to be *that* good. Most people in sales are pleased with a success rate that is far less than that. But I didn't tell her this, and I don't plan to!

Another thing people in sales often fret about is market saturation. Am I too late? They look at someone like Wilburn Smith, who started almost twenty years ago, and say, "Boy, I wish I got in when Wilburn did!" And I tell them, "No, you don't. Believe me!" Readers who closely followed all the ups and downs recounted in chapter 6 will know what I'm talking about.

For Pre-Paid Legal, the best time is now—not twenty years ago or two years from now. This business is taking off. As for saturation? We've operated in Oklahoma for nearly thirty years and as soon as we get the last 98 percent of this market sewn up, it'll be saturated! In Texas, all we need is another 99.9 percent. And now we have opened up Canada. Even Ada, Oklahoma, is not saturated!

One thing you'll never see me do is dangle promises of vast, overnight riches in front of people who think about joining our business. This is hard but genuine and rewarding work. What I will point out is that in America, only about 1 percent of the population earns more than $100,000 a year, and we've got a lot of people making $100,000 a year and more.

The Yes! Man

I'd like to introduce you to some of them—and there's no better person to start with than Wilburn Smith. The next time you face a big disappointment or find your dream shattered, go talk to Wilburn. His simple dream was to own an IGA grocery store up in his hometown of Holdenville, Oklahoma, some thirty-eight miles from Ada. That dream was shattered. Today, he's president of our company!

He put twenty years into the grocery and convenience-store business, working his way up to a $30,000 manager's salary at the very IGA store he wanted to buy. What kept Wilburn going was a promise from the owner that he would sell it to Wilburn upon his retirement.

When the time came, the owner turned around and sold it to someone else.

Wilburn was devastated, but he was lucky to have a cousin, Mike Smith, who was one of the first salesmen I ever hired at Pre-Paid Legal. "Mike tried to talk me into selling Pre-Paid," Wilburn recalls. "It was 1980 and back then, the company wasn't into network marketing yet. You just got commissions on your sales.

"Pre-Paid gave me a week of training and, boy, did I need it. There was a rule that you had to sign up twenty-five individual members before they'd let you call on a group. That was a good thing, because I was scared to death!"

Once Wilburn made the necessary individual sales, Mike took him along as part of a team that was to call on the Oklahoma City Fire Department. The presentations to groups of firefighters were done in pairs, so Wilburn was able to keep his nervousness under control.

But on the evening of the first day of the presentations, he was shocked to discover that Mike had been called away. He alone would have to make the pitches the next day. "I was so scared," Wilburn recalls, "that I drove around the fire station for thirty minutes. Then I just sat there in my car for another thirty minutes."

But when he finally got up the nerve to go into the station, he was in for a pleasant surprise. No matter how afraid and inexperienced, he made the sales! His first presentation was to four firemen. Two were already members and he signed up the other two. By the end of the week, he signed forty-seven more.

Cousin Mike was impressed, but he wanted to take one more look at Wilburn. "He put me in a room with six prospects and peeked in through the door while I made my pitch," Wilburn says. "I sold all six of them! Right after that meeting, Mike told me, 'You don't need me anymore. I'm going back to Ada.'"

Even so, the first year was tough for Wilburn Smith. The $25,000 he made was a cut in pay from IGA. But then a funny thing started happening. His income began to double from year to year. During his second year with us, Wilburn made $50,000, and it doubled again in the third year, to $100,000. That was especially big money back in 1982, and it's nothing to sneeze at today.

And all this was before we'd even introduced network marketing to our business. Once that happened, Wilburn's income stopped doubling and started tripling! "From August 1983 to the end of 1984, my income tripled to $300,000—thanks to the efforts of the people I brought into this business."

None of this happened by luck or accident. It happened because Wilburn is very good at what he does and works very, very hard. He has held just about every position there is at Pre-Paid Legal and has stuck with it no matter what. That includes the time in the mid- to late-'80s when, thanks to network marketing, we were so successful in writing new business that we just plain ran out of money. I faced a terrible choice—either stop paying advance commissions for awhile or go bankrupt. We suspended the commissions for a time and lost most of our sales force—but not Wilburn!

In fact, after that terrible ordeal, I tapped Wilburn to rebuild our sales force. Armed with a new marketing plan, he was off to the races, and Pre-Paid was back on track, growing faster than ever. Wilburn says that the best advice for success he has ever received and given is simple: "Figure out what you do best and do a whole lot of it." He did a whole lot of it in the early 1990s as Pre-Paid's vice president of marketing.

Wilburn loves to tell the story of what happened next:

"It was a Friday evening and Carol and I were dropping Harland and Shirley off at the airport after dinner. As they got out of the car, Harland said, 'If I could give you some really good news, could you be in my office at 8:00 A.M. next Tuesday morning?' I said yes. He called me in with Randy Harp and handed me a press release they wanted to put out, announcing that I was going to be the new president of Pre-Paid Legal Services.

"As my mouth dropped open, Harland asked me how I felt about it. I said, 'It makes me really happy, but what about my compensation?' And he replied, 'Well, you're sure as hell not going to get a raise!'

"In fact, I was making plenty of money from the organization I had built. Harland is one man who absolutely doesn't care how much money you make. If you produce—and production is what it's all about with me—the sky is the limit and that's just fine with him.

"I believe I was chosen to be president because I relate to the people in the sales force, and they relate to me. I've been there and done that. I've gone out there and done what they are trying to do. My approach with our salespeople is to mix tough love and sympathy. I've made every mistake there is to make and if I can keep them from making some of the same ones, Pre-Paid will continue to grow."

Wilburn makes fantastic predictions all the time about our potential for growth. I remember the day not too long ago when he came into the office with that day's edition of *USA Today*, which reported that the world's population had just reached the six billion milestone. And Wilburn said, "Yes!" Then someone pointed out to him that the article also said that there are 170,000 babies born in the United States every single day. And again, Wilburn said, "Yes! We'll never run out of prospects. Never!"

Wilburn's optimism is amazing, especially when you consider that we came so close to losing him. Three years ago, right before Thanksgiving, doctors found a malignant tumor in his bile duct and the cancer had spread to vital organs.

At best, Wilburn had a 50-50 chance to make it, but those odds plunged when he was rushed back to the hospital with internal bleeding after his first surgery. The doctors warned Carol to prepare for the worst. We were in Branson, Missouri, at the time, with hundreds of our top salespeople and their families. We organized a nationwide prayer chain for Wilburn that extended coast to coast.

Wilburn credits the power of prayer with saving his life. Today he's doing fine, happily invoking that one word that sums up his entire attitude toward life: "Yes!" He says: "I'm living my dream now. Pre-Paid Legal has given me so much—and I have a lot to give back to others who join our company."

Best of the Best

Our Platinum executive directors are the best of the best, the very top achievers in the Pre-Paid Legal business. Let's take a look at where they came from and how they did it.

Kevin Rhea (Platinum 4)

Pre-Paid Legal is a full-time venture for Kevin Rhea of Waco, Texas. He joined the business as a result of the company's October 1998 acquisition of The People's Network (TPN). "Pre-Paid Legal is a unique company with an enormous amount of credibility and financial stability," says Kevin. "Being in the early stages of growth with a valuable product that has virtually no competition and less than 2 percent market penetration, PPL has yet to realize its full potential."

Knowing he would not enjoy the restrictions of an employer or the corporate structure, Kevin became involved in network marketing soon after graduating from college. "This business has allowed me to make a significant monthly income at twenty-seven years of age that will only continue to grow. I'm able to make more money in a month than most people make in an entire year," Kevin explains. "This business gives me the ability to work when I want or to take off at a minute's notice to be with my wife, Leslie, our family, and our friends. It's great to know I have control of my own time and my own destiny."

Kevin identifies three keys to success in the Pre-Paid Legal business:

"First, exposure is everything. You have to expose PPL to as many people as possible.

"Second, fortune is in the follow-up. You will never know if someone is interested if you don't follow up. Many associates 'leave money on the table' by failing to do so.

"Third, work with the willing. Don't waste your time dragging associates across the finish line if they do not want to do what it takes to be successful."

Kevin encourages all associates to, first, make a one-year commitment to the business and, second, be consistent. "It's a marathon, not a sprint," he explains. "During the first year, attend as many seminars and opportunity meetings as you can. Treat PPL like a business and not just a hobby.

"You'll get out of it exactly what you put into it," concludes Kevin—one of our best Pre-paid Legal success stories.

Dave Savula (Platinum 4)

Dave and Bev Savula of Dawsonville, Georgia, first purchased a Pre-Paid Legal membership twelve years ago, but it wasn't until 1992 that they joined the business as associates. As part owners of a telephone resale business, the Savulas knew how to spot a service whose time had come. "It's not a question of whether you're going to own a Pre-Paid plan, it's when," predicts Dave.

Today, eight years after joining the business, the Savulas rank as our top money earners, with an organization that numbers in the hundreds of thousands.

"We not only help ourselves with this business," Dave observes, "but we also help others to a better way of life. We have developed a long list of friends to share time with."

201

Given their remarkable success, Dave and Bev are eagerly sought after for advice and support. "Be consistent at what you do, keep it simple, and your business will grow," Dave counsels. Bev observes: "Pre-Paid Legal is like life. You only get what you give. If you give 100 percent, you get back 100 percent; give only 10 percent, and you get 10 percent.

"Your business depends on you! You and you alone are responsible for your success or failure!"

Ken Moore (Platinum 3)

Before their involvement with Pre-Paid Legal, Ken and Shirlene Moore of Ada, Oklahoma, already owned two businesses—a private detective agency and a meat-packing plant. But they were looking for a career change and the company fit the bill.

"Having already bought a Pre-Paid membership and being happy with the service, we asked to look at the marketing plan and found that it offered good advance money and even better renewal income. That's what really caught our attention!" Ken remembers.

Ken and Shirlene became associates in 1984. "We began by working the business part-time," Ken says. "But soon we realized the potential.

"In our first six months we made $48,600, marketing what was then a $10 membership. That's the least amount we ever made in a six-month period."

Now Ken and Shirlene tell us that they make in excess of $30,000 a month! The Moores advise associates to ask prospects if they can be financially secure in their present jobs. "When they say no," Ken reveals, "simply respond, 'Mr. or Mrs. Prospect, if I can show you that opportunity, then you owe it to yourself to give me thirty minutes of your time, don't you think?'"

Today Ken is not only a Platinum 3 executive director, he is our vice president of marketing in charge of group sales, which I believe will lead Pre-Paid Legal to explosive growth in this new decade. Ken and Shirlene have a daughter, Shana, and a son, Randy, who, as you will learn later, represents a tremendous Pre-Paid Legal success story in his own right!

Fran Alexander (Platinum 2)

When Fran Alexander of Corona, California, met her husband, Woody, she was a single mother with six children. She knew firsthand what it was like to be unable to afford attorney fees, yet not to qualify for legal aid. "After hearing a brief presentation, I realized that everyone I knew needed this service and they didn't even know it was available," she explains.

Fran and Woody got off to a great start, selling more than 32,000 memberships during a six-year period in the mid-1980s. But then a series of problems arose.

A son was about to lose his business and couldn't afford any office help. Fran volunteered to help him out. Then, Woody's mother became ill, and Woody chose to care for her rather than put her in a home. Around the same time, a grandson had a serious accident—and the Alexanders spent many nights by his side in the hospital.

"During all of this, we got a check every month from the renewal income on memberships written since 1983," Fran points out. "Do you know of any company that would allow you to take time off for three years, pay you every month, and then give you back your same position when you returned?"

When they did return, they built their business with a vengeance, enlisting tens of thousands of associates who together signed up hundreds of thousands of Pre-Paid memberships. Fran declares that she's not finished building the business but enjoys spending time with the couple's eight children and nineteen grandchildren, sometimes on the Alexander yacht, appropriately named "The Recruiter." "We're living the life that most people only dream of!" Fran exclaims.

Mark Brown (Platinum 2 and Regional Vice President, Texas)

"I have never been part of or joined another multilevel or network marketing company," says Mark Brown, a former printer from Weatherford, Texas. "I always made a great effort to stay away from them.

"Everyone I did printing for tried to recruit me, but Pre-Paid Legal was different. I have never seen a product that made so much sense or one that hit me like this one did."

Mark and his father had owned and operated a printing business together for fifteen years, but when his dad died in 1994, it just wasn't the same. Mark wanted to do something different—and that's when he discovered Pre-Paid.

Within two months he sold his business and began marketing Pre-Paid full time. "Whatever I got into, I didn't ever want to dread going to work. I know so many people who do," he observes. "With Pre-Paid, I honestly can't wait to work at this each day!"

And the results show. With his wife, Denise, by his side, Mark Brown has an organization that spreads throughout thirty-five states and has well over 100,000 customer-members. He is regional vice president for Texas and, instead of being in the printing business, he's practically printing money, earning around $40,000 each month!

Mike and Michael Dorsey (Platinum 2)

It's great to see such a successful father/son team in our business—and we've got that in Mike and Michael Dorsey of Georgia.

Mike and his wife, Lola, had been Pre-Paid Legal members since the 1980s, so they knew the value of the product. Until five years ago, Mike was in sales management and his son, Michael, owned a successful landscaping company. Both had been involved in other network marketing companies on a part-time basis. Once they got into Pre-Paid, however, it has been full time all the way.

"Anyone can do this business," they say. "The only way you can fail is not to try." The Dorseys advise new associates to begin by making a list of their top ten prospects and then setting up three-way calls with them.

Michael, who lives in Cumming, Georgia, with his wife, Amy, and daughter Alexis, believes that Pre-Paid Legal has allowed him to grow personally. He now speaks in front of large audiences—"something I could never imagine myself doing before!"

"One of the best things about this business," the Dorseys say, "is that it lets you build up residual income to enjoy for many years to come."

Mildred Baker (Platinum)

Millie and Bake Baker of Tulsa, Oklahoma, were recruited into our business fourteen years ago and today have a strong organization in twelve states.

Before Pre-Paid Legal, Millie was a bank teller and a director of local and state beauty pageants. She now concentrates on working her group accounts, while Bake, a former landscaper and insurance agent, works on recruiting new associates.

As good as the income can be (and it is, for the Bakers!), Millie reminds us that hard work is the key to success in this business. So is being persistent! "It's amazing what you can accomplish by hard work and not taking 'no' for an answer," she says.

"When I do a presentation, I always try to put myself in the position of whomever I am talking to. You relate the service to the particular group you are in front of, whether it is schoolteachers or police officers."

Their formula for success can be summed up simply: "Work hard and stay focused, make it fun, and do it as a team—and, above all, don't give up!"

Brian Carruthers (Platinum)

Before Pre-Paid Legal, Brian Carruthers of Rockville, Maryland, was in real estate, but he walked away from a family-owned real estate company with twenty-one branch offices to become a full-time network marketer.

"I used to have a great income, but the lifestyle that I sacrificed to achieve the financial gain just wasn't worth it," he explains. Today, not even thirty, Brian enjoys the kind of lifestyle most people only dream of, working on his own terms from his home and earning a great income.

Unlike others, Brian didn't have to be sold on network marketing. He studied the industry closely and knew it was for him. But he wasn't convinced that Pre-Paid Legal was the right vehicle. "I found myself looking for that network marketing deal I could get into at the right time and ride the wave into the six-figure income promised land," Brian explains. "I never thought in a million years that after all my searching and trying, I would find that vehicle in a company that's been around for twenty-eight years. But it didn't take me long to realize that momentum has begun and critical mass will hit in the near future," he says.

"Pre-Paid has virtually no competition, less than one out of a hundred people have our product, and the compensation plan is so strong that a brand-new person can come into the business and make about $1,000 on their first day by signing up less than a dozen customers. That's what will attract the novice networkers and keep them in the game.

"I attribute my success to this kind of highly duplicable system."

Yvetta Collins (Platinum)

Yvetta Collins of Desoto, Texas, was an investment officer for a large bank before joining Pre-Paid Legal. Her husband, Kelvin, convinced her to go to a sales presentation and both were dubious as the meeting got underway. But soon they began to see "that the market was totally untapped, unlike the insurance and investment fields."

Within three months, the Collinses were in the business full time and it took only thirteen months for them to become executive directors. In just six months, they matched their income from their previous jobs.

No wonder Yvetta has concluded: "This is the most incredible business opportunity in America. I make enough money so that all six children can go to private school. That was one of my dreams come true. With Pre-Paid Legal, I can be there when my kids get home from school each day."

Yvetta stresses that the key to success is to "teach your recruits to duplicate themselves. You don't build sales; you build people and people build sales."

Joe and Barbara Dameron (Platinum and Regional Vice President, North Carolina)

Joe Dameron says he has looked for the Pre-Paid Legal opportunity for twenty years.

"After being involved with other network marketing companies where you had to stock products, maintain production, and pay your downline, I knew when I saw this fabulous product and commission schedule that this was the one for me."

His wife, Barbara, introduced Joe to the opportunity and the product. Who introduced it to her is still a mystery. "Someone left an audiotape and a product brochure at our insurance office," Joe recalls. "After several months Barbara finally looked at it, and she thought it would be a great product to offer to our insurance clients."

When they became involved with Pre-Paid Legal, Joe says he was convinced that he could become a millionaire with the company. "I immediately began faxing and calling friends, relatives, and prior business associates and sharing the opportunity with them," he says. "I found out immediately that if you help enough people get what they want in life, you can have anything you want.

"We have been able to help others as well as ourselves," Joe explains. "We bought a new Suburban and paid cash for it. We've never done anything like that before. We also bought a new boat, remodeled our home, and traveled.

"The people who laughed at us in the beginning have changed their attitude about PPL and our little home-based business," he adds. "Now they're coming to us for information."

And Pre-Paid Legal is definitely a family affair for the Damerons of Hubert, North Carolina. All three of their children are Pre-Paid directors!

Toby Cutberth (Platinum)

Toby Cutberth of Grass Valley, California, has always understood what it means to be a hard worker. As an underground, hard-rock gold miner like his father, he learned never to take success for granted. Later, his philosophy would lead him to a high-level executive position that placed him in the top 1 percent of income earners in America.

Today, Toby and his wife, Bonnie, work their Pre-Paid Legal business part-time. Even so, they made it to the executive director level in just eighteen months, bringing in a six-figure income from their part-time business.

"Share it with a few people, then commit to helping them," advises Toby. He says his best recruiting periods are when he and his wife meet with likely prospects face-to-face. "The reason we love network marketing so much is the face-to-face contact with people," he says. "It's the opportunity to help people get started on better lives for themselves."

The Cutberths have used their sizable Pre-Paid Legal income to build a secure retirement fund. But that's not all the building they have done. Pre-Paid also paid for the 6,000-square-foot dream home they built in the foothills of the Sierra Nevadas!

Jae Hoglund (Platinum)

Before joining Pre-Paid Legal, Jae Hoglund of Butler, Pennsylvania, owned and operated an executive search firm specializing in mid- to upper-level management personnel. He therefore had a firsthand view of the corporate rat race and the changes in traditional employment that were leading many to start their own home-based businesses.

Initially interested in offering PPL to clients as a benefit for their employees, Jae soon realized that the power of renewal-based marketing and networking was much more far-reaching. Jae and his wife, Jackie, thought that a part-time Pre-Paid business might help defray college costs for their children but "when we started seeing $500 a week, that got my attention," he recalls. When the checks started coming in at an average of $500 a day, Jae was convinced to work the business full-time!

"We had the product ourselves for ten years. I knew it worked and knew everyone needed it. Since my background was in recruiting, I knew I could attract new associates into our opportunity," Jae explains.

What Jae appreciates most is the opportunity to develop his own retirement income with no risk of corporate downsizing. And there's something more: "Strong business relationships have developed into strong personal relationships, thanks to this business. Being able to work with people and actually help them achieve their dreams is more than financially rewarding."

Joe Lemire (Platinum and Regional Vice President, Ohio)

Joe and Ruth Lemire of Akron, Ohio, call themselves gamblers and dream seekers. "Over the past thirty years, my wife and I have worked and searched for the lifestyle that would provide for us, as well as nurture our family," Joe says. "We've worked hard and made the best of many an opportunity during those years, knowing that someday we would hit the jackpot, and along came Pre-Paid Legal."

Joe was involved in the health insurance business and made a very healthy income when he and Ruth bought a Pre-Paid membership in 1993. They used the service several times and were very impressed.

The quality of the service moved the Lemires to sign up as associates. They began to work the business on a part-time basis, but within a year, they were full-timers.

"When my part-time income from Pre-Paid started to equal my full-time income in insurance, that's when we reset our goals," Joe explains.

"We have a great team, without whom we would not have moved along as we have," say the Lemires. "Our goal now is helping our entire team realize the same good fortune we have!"

Joe and Ruth advise new recruits to "set your goals and write them down, then go to work and never quit." The best way to recruit, says Joe, is "simply to talk to lots of people every day. I believe this opportunity is the average person's best chance to earn a great deal of money."

Today, the Lemires say they make more money than they can spend, but the best part of their business is the freedom to travel and to write business almost anywhere they want.

"Our whole family is involved as members or associates," Joe proudly reports. "Two of our sons, Mike and

Paul, are area coordinators. As soon as our four grand-children are old enough, they'll be involved, too!"

Mike and Steve Melia (Platinum)

The Melia brothers have a "rags-to-riches" story to tell. They used to live in their sister's attic and shared a GEO Metro for transportation. But they put up with those conditions while building their business because they had become fed up with failing to achieve their financial goals in the traditional working world.

"Since I was eleven years old, my goal was to become a millionaire," says Steve. "My brother was eighteen years older than me and sort of a pioneer. He started a natural foods outlet on Long Island in 1976 and later got involved in the seminar industry in the early '80s. I became his partner when I was twenty-four."

Before joining forces with his brother, Steve worked at door-to-door sales and later did stand-up comedy in New York City. "Pre-Paid Legal sort of found us," Mike recalls. "Jeff Olson and Eric Worre of TPN were our mentors, and they showed us how to use the basic ideas and strategies to build an international sales force."

"We found it incredible that Pre-Paid was a mature company that had real traction in the marketplace," Steve adds. "Even more than that, it had a much needed product that had already proved successful in Europe."

Mike tells us, "One of the greatest results I've been able to achieve is to send my daughter Jessica to the university of her choice. Thank God for Pre-Paid Legal." Mike has three other children, two of whom are PPL associates.

"For the new associates," Steve offers, "I recommend doing what we did. Learn the systems that the company promotes and use those systems. Take advantage of the tools—the audios, the videos, and the Web site. It's an exposure game. Massive exposure means massive results.

"We believe in thinking big," Steve concludes. "It's better to have big goals than small ones. Pre-Paid Legal is like a rocket ship to the moon. Mike and I are glad to be along for the ride."

Randy and Pat Moore (Platinum and Regional Vice President, Oklahoma)

Just like me, Randy Moore was led to Pre-Paid Legal by a car crash.

Working as an Oklahoma highway patrolman, Randy had engaged in a high-speed pursuit that left him seriously injured. During his recuperation, his father, Ken Moore, introduced him to Pre-Paid's business opportunity.

"My Dad, who is the company's executive vice president of group marketing, recruited me," Randy says. "He showed me a way to make money that would be a lot less hazardous to my health!"

Randy had made $3,000 a month with the Oklahoma Highway Patrol after seventeen years of service.

His wife, Pat, brought home another $1,000 from real estate sales. Now Randy works the Pre-Paid Legal business part-time, while Pat does it full-time. "My old salary couldn't compare to the money I made with PPL," he reports. "Also, this was a way that I felt I could continue to help others. I made a commitment right then and there to become a Pre-Paid associate.

"People really cannot afford to do without the product," Randy continues. "It is something that everyone needs, everyone wants, and is very affordable. I always assume the sale!"

Randy and Pat and their three children live in Durant, Oklahoma. Randy's bottom line is what it has always been—service. "My whole life has been dedicated to the service of others," Randy says, "first in the United States Marine Corps, then as a state trooper, and now as an executive director with Pre-Paid Legal."

Don Whigham (Platinum)

Be a starmaker—that's Don Whigham's philosophy. "I work closely with those who are willing to work hard," says the Plano, Texas, resident. That determination to work with winners brings him a six-figure annual income, thanks to Pre-Paid Legal.

Before Pre-Paid, Don had his own accounting and computer services business. "I searched for over a year for a strong service network marketing company that had not yet hit momentum," Don explains. "That was hard to find.

"I had built large organizations with start-up companies only to see them crumble. I'm glad to be with PPL. This is an opportunity with a long-term future. With 86 percent of all businesses failing in three years, it's important to hook up with a proven company."

Don and his wife, Phyllis, are particularly proud that one of their two children is also building a Pre-Paid Legal business—another of the many examples of the family approach to our business.

Success As Big As America

And now, meet our regional vice presidents. These men and women have not only built successful network marketing organizations, they also hold the important responsibility of making sure that Pre-Paid Legal grows in sales and recruiting in every state and Canada.

Kathy Aaron (Montana)

"My success story is eight years in the making," says Kathy Aaron of Bozeman, Montana. "It's simply a matter of perseverance and doing the right things. Over the past eight years I have developed relationships with people who are more to me than just business acquaintances.

Because of these relationships, we work as a team to help everyone reach the level of success he or she desires. My success is the team."

It's the product that makes Pre-Paid Legal so strong in Kathy's eyes. "I like the fact that everyone can make a living by simply offering a valuable product," she says. "A $25 sale, generating significant commissions, is a built-in motivator for anyone."

For Kathy, formerly in real estate, it motivated her to the level of executive director in just one month!

"PPL has given me the opportunity to live the lifestyle I have dreamed of—to live in Montana and build a business all over the country. To have the freedom to choose what I do, and when and with whom to do it, is glorious," she says. "PPL allows me to spend time with my family and work my business at the same time, without the stress of traditional business."

Kathy says she is amazed at how positive everyone is about Pre-Paid Legal. "People who would usually shy away from network marketing are drawn to Pre-Paid Legal more than to any company I've seen," she adds.

Kathy asks questions to help her prospects understand the value of the product and the magnitude of the business opportunity. She tells new recruits to "get started immediately! Do something in your first forty-eight hours with your sponsor and get plugged in. Get close to the fire by receiving information as soon as possible."

218

Daniel and Angie Abbott (Arkansas)

When Angie Abbott was eighteen years old, her parents, Larry and Mary King, became her Pre-Paid Legal sponsors.

"I grew up hearing the success stories and seeing what Pre-Paid Legal could do for the middle-income family in America," she remembers. "Pre-Paid Legal has been a part of our family for more than sixteen years. Watching your parents become successful at something they love to do has been great! What is so exciting now is that we have had the same opportunity."

Daniel's introduction to Pre-Paid Legal was through Angie. "He married into the Pre-Paid family business," Angie says.

Before Pre-Paid, Daniel was a cable technician and Angie taught school. The business has now enabled them to buy a new home in Walnut Ridge, Arkansas. In September 1998, Daniel suffered a heart attack and was unable to work for two months. "Financially, it was nice to know that we didn't have to worry," Angie explains. "The money just kept coming in!"

Theresa and Frank AuCoin (South Carolina)

Theresa AuCoin's professional background is teaching. She has a master's degree in three areas of education and has taught special education for eight years. Frank's background is street-smart business. The Charleston couple

219

started a chain of bookstores that has been sold and a nutrition business that also has been sold. Most recently, they franchised a chain of sign businesses across the Southeast.

It was after this successful track record that the Au-Coins jumped at the Pre-Paid legal opportunity and—no surprise—success has come again!

"Pre-Paid Legal is not a get rich quick deal," Frank says. "But it is a get rich plan that actually works." Theresa adds, "Making money has always been a game to me. The only thing that really matters in playing the game are the people along the way. What makes Pre-Paid so much fun is that we get to work with the most positive, self-motivated, moving-forward type of people!"

The AuCoins have some good advice for aspiring associates: "We strive for our business to be balanced. We have a lot of associates doing group sales and others who are seriously into the network marketing side of the business.

"Our advice is to do two things for sure. Work the events. That means, be at every event. Get good at promoting them and getting guests and associates to attend. Events are the heartbeat of the business.

"And, simply commit to being here for at least three years. Not one of the businesses that we built in the past was really very profitable until the third year.

"The nice thing—and the bad thing—about PPL is that there is very little financial commitment and practically no overhead. It's great, because who wants all of that? It's bad, because it's easy not to take it seriously and not to make the commitment with so little on the line, financially," Theresa adds.

"I suggest you write out a check to My Financial Future for $249,000 and tape it to your mirror or your desk. Work this business as if you made that kind of financial commitment. Wouldn't you be able to make a serious three-year commitment with that investment? The return here can be much greater financially than in any other business we know of—if you make the commitment."

John and Janice Biro (Florida, South)

When someone handed John Biro a Pre-Paid Legal videotape to review, it took him two months to find the time to sit down and watch it. But once he did, it took him no time at all to make a decision. He signed up as an associate the very next day.

"This service is great!" John says. "There are no products, no inventory, no minimums, very low start-up costs, unlimited income potential, and renewal income potential."

His Pre-Paid Legal business is still a part-time venture for John, who continues to manage a country club. But his wife, Janice, who worked in the hospitality industry, can now afford to stay home, care for the couple's daughter, and oversee home renovations funded by their PPL income.

"When I started my PPL business, I had three strikes against me," John remembers. "I had no sales experience.

I had no insurance experience. And I had no networking experience. It took four months for me to make my first sale. I was presenting the product but just not asking for the check. After seven months and only fifteen organizational sales, I made every mistake possible, but I finally figured it out."

Today John and Janice have a rapidly growing organization that has tapped into Pompano Beach's large retirement community.

"A retired neighbor asked me what I was working on early in the morning and late at night," John recalls. "I was vague about it because I didn't think he'd be interested. Then he told me, 'People think I'm retired. I'm never going to retire. Tell me what you're doing.' I showed him, and he signed up and now has more than 300 associates and 1,000 membership sales in his downline. Don't prejudge people!"

John says the best thing about the PPL business is not the great money, it's "helping my organization across the United States reach their goals. If I can help them reach their goals, then my goals are achieved!"

Charlie Brown (West Virginia)

"When people ask me if Pre-Paid Legal is a hard business to be in, I can't help smiling," says Charlie Brown, our regional vice president for West Virginia. "I tell them to look under their kitchen table and imagine that they are crawling under it and under the ground a few miles. It is black and cold and wet. The ceiling keeps falling down on you and danger is everywhere. You have to fight the rats for your lunch bucket and stay there for eight hours a day."

You've probably guessed that Charlie was a coal miner before joining Pre-Paid. When he had had enough of that, he tried the insurance business and was pretty good at it, but making a decent living was no cakewalk. "Even so, I stuck it out for many years," says Charlie. "I built a sizable sales force when suddenly my company was sold. The corporate politics started and agents began drifting away. I got completely burned out."

In late 1993, Joe Lemire called Charlie and asked him to consider Pre-Paid. Because Joe was a friend, Charlie drove all the way to Columbus, Ohio, to attend a presentation. "My business partner and I were the only ones there. I was not impressed," Charlie recalls. "I told Joe I wasn't interested."

But Joe kept coming after Charlie. "Finally, I said yes just to keep him from bothering me!"

Within three months Charlie was successful enough to make Pre-Paid his full-time occupation. In just over three years he reached the executive director level. It's a night and day difference from his jobs in the coal mine and the insurance business, Charlie observes. "Let me tell you about the change in money and the change in freedom. For the first time I have money left over after I pay my bills each month. To me, that means just about everything. I can go on vacation whenever I want and don't have to ask any boss. And if I'm sick, I can stay home and get well and not worry about the money not coming in. It all comes down to *freedom.*"

David and Renea Brued (Oregon)

"It didn't take long to figure out that this was an opportunity of a lifetime and my family's future," says David Brued of Lake Oswego, Oregon, who became a full-time Pre-Paid Legal associate on the first day he signed up.

"Why dabble with your future?" he asks. "I always found myself getting into me-too industries like telecommunications and computer software. I never did very well in any of them.

"As an entrepreneur, I always kept my ear to the ground," David says. "But I had never heard of PPL. If I had never heard of it, then there must be a lot of other people who never heard of it. I like the fact that I don't have to sell. All I have to do is share a story and most people choose to participate. What's not to like?"

That's not to say that success comes easily or automatically!

In his first month David says he was caught up with "paralysis by analysis," as he "studied myself to death. I quickly realized that the company didn't pay me for activity. It paid for results. That's when I went out and started talking to people and, much to my surprise, they signed up. That was a great boost to my confidence."

One of the things David likes most about our business is that it's a "people helping people business. And it gives me peace of mind knowing that a little hard work and the PPL opportunity will afford me the opportunity to spend quality time with Renea and our son Austin—and take care of their future at the same time."

Ted and Olga Burke (Nevada)

Before Pre-Paid Legal, Ted Burke of Las Vegas worked as a police officer. His wife was a bank auditor. He had to be invited to a Pre-Paid Legal opportunity meeting six times before he finally went!

"I was invited six times—so for those of you who invited a guest who didn't show up, don't give up! Persistence is the key to success," Ted counsels.

As a police officer, Ted made about $3,200 a month. His job and Olga's bank job "absorbed all our time and provided inadequate compensation. PPL allowed us to escape from that rut and improve the lifestyle of our whole family."

Now the Burkes enjoy a six-figure income with their full-time Pre-Paid Legal business. They like the fact that their business allows them to work together and spend quality time with each other. Ted's favorite aspect of PPL is "the ability to operate our own business without the paperwork generally associated with business ownership."

Greg and Shannon Darragh
(British Columbia)

After almost twenty-five combined years in the insurance industry, Greg and Shannon Darragh of Kelowna, British Columbia, learned from personal experience as well as observation that the door to justice was too costly to walk through for average Canadians.

They first learned about Pre-Paid Legal by reading an August 1997 article in *Success* magazine. "We immediately knew this was the company that would help Canadians gain affordable access to the legal system. This was a product and an opportunity whose time had come," Greg and Shannon explain.

"One of the philosophies we practiced throughout our careers is not to reinvent the wheel. We saw Pre-Paid become a success in the United States and knew the same formula would work in Canada. We were just elated when Pre-Paid opened for business here."

Now the Darraghs enjoy the time they spend with their son Zack in their home in British Columbia's beautiful wine country. "Pre-Paid Legal has fulfilled a large part of our dream to have affordable access to the Canadian legal system," they tell us.

"But we believe the best is yet to come for everyone who either has a Pre-Paid membership or who takes advantage of this incredible business opportunity here in Canada."

Reynold and Lorraine Diaz
(New York, South)

"Believe you can do it." It's simple advice, but it has taken Reynold and Lorraine Diaz of Brooklyn a long way in a very short time. In Reynold's first five months with the company, he personally trained more than 500 associates. In his first year, his organization signed up 20,000 members.

"I am totally committed," he says. "Pre-Paid Legal is my full-time career."

Reynold believes in sharing information about Pre-Paid with everyone who needs legal services and "not too many people know about it yet."

So what does Reynold say to people who don't believe?

"Take a second look," he says. Hear it from someone else in the business because usually it's not the message but the messenger. Don't sell yourself short. Look at it again just one more time.

"It all comes down to teamwork and a strong belief that what you are doing is right and that there's a need for it," Reynold advises.

"My dream and the dream of my associates is to work with the 'greedys' and not the 'needys.'" Reynold defines the "greedys" as those who want more money and a better life and are willing to work for it and make it happen. He says the "needys" are those who want the same things but don't have the desire or drive to make it happen for themselves. They want others to do the work for them.

"This is not a company that promises, but one that delivers," concludes Reynold.

George and Merrily Ford
(Pennsylvania, West)

Before starting their Pre-Paid Legal business, George Ford of Pittsburgh had owned and operated a fireplace company for twenty-two years. Merrily had always been a full-time mom. Now they say, "We're making history. Someday, Pre-Paid Legal will be a story you'll tell your grandchildren. Either you'll tell them about the great opportunity you missed or you'll say—this is how grandpa made all his money!"

It took the Fords all of six months to make the executive director level. "The Pre-Paid marketing plan is so friendly to part-time people," they explain. "Their commissions are not dependent on maintaining a certain amount of volume or purchasing unwanted inventory every month. Everyone gets paid for his or her performance."

Income is only part of the reward the Fords believe they reap from PPL. "Equally as important as the money we earn are the wonderful friends we've made—upline, downline, and sideline. People working together as a team make it all worthwhile!"

228

Desmond Gibson (Connecticut)

"It has been rightly stated that success is not a destination but a journey. And in my journey of twenty-five years of being self-employed, I can safely say that I have found the vehicle that will make my success dreams become a reality," says Desmond Gibson of Brooklyn, New York.

Desmond says he's a 100-percent full-time PPL associate, having been introduced to the business by his good friend Ron Diaz. He became an executive director in just eight months, "which gave me the chance to be financially independent, marketing a much-needed service and helping others do the same."

Before Pre-Paid, Desmond was a marketing and training director for a health and nutrition company. PPL has allowed him to triple his old income, giving him and his wife, Patricia, the financial freedom to care for and spend more time with their four children.

Desmond reflects on the most frustrating occurrence for people in sales—rejection. "The potential member/customer only needs more information," is the positive attitude he takes. In fact, one rejection was from a young college professor who said he had no interest in marketing anything. Desmond did not give up but instead took the time and incurred the cost to send overnight some additional materials. The professor, impressed by the trouble and expense Desmond went to, reviewed the materials carefully, decided to sign up, and three months later reached the executive director level!

Desmond believes that the best way to succeed is to "do less talking and more showing. Always remember that the eye is a better pupil than the ear. Show and explain the product. Show and explain the marketing plan. Being paid every day through direct deposit is unique!"

Les and Lorie Harrell (Colorado)

Les and Lorie Harrell of Littleton, Colorado, enjoyed a great income in the custom jewelry and repair business. "But we did not have any time to spend with our family," Les remembers. "Being in the retail business, the holidays are the worst. When most families got together and enjoyed each other's company, we worked. In the nine years we were married before joining PPL, something as simple as decorating the Christmas tree was not done as a family. Instead, Lorie did it by herself and I worked."

Now, with Pre-Paid Legal, not only do the Harrellses earn a higher income; "We have the ability to spend time together as a family," says Lorie.

Les and Lorie were sold on the Pre-Paid opportunity when they directly experienced the value of their membership. "After a personal experience in which it worked for us, we looked at the business side of PPL. It just made sense to us that this was something we could be passionate about and help others with, while providing for our family," they explain.

"Pre-Paid Legal has changed the way we live," say Les and Lorie. "We get to choose how we spend our days now. We have three boys and they get a lot of our time and attention now. It is so rewarding to be the parent who helps out in the classroom and gets to go on field trips. We cannot imagine doing anything else.

"Helping people, watching people grow through the development of their business, and living the life we choose to live. It just doesn't get any better than this!"

Jack Hawk (Iowa)

Six years ago, when Jack Hawk was all of twenty-five years old, he thought he already had everything he wanted out of life. He and a partner had built a respectable insurance business, owning three agencies in Kansas City, St. Louis, and his hometown, Omaha, Nebraska.

But something was missing. "I spent every waking moment either on the road, visiting one of our offices, in an insurance appointment, dealing with clients, hiring employees, training agents and staff, or doing payroll for thirty employees," Jack says. "I had no time for my wife and three young children."

Then Jack ran into business problems that brought crushing legal bills. He ended up closing his insurance business and found himself $500,000 in debt. "I was depressed and felt like a failure," he reports.

But in the fall of 1996 while on a family trip to Denver, Jack decided to look up an old friend who might have some ideas as to what he could do next. They connected and Jack was introduced to Pre-Paid Legal. "I was hooked," Jack reports. "I signed my associate agreement on September 19, 1996. My first few checks went to pay attorney fees from my bankruptcy."

That was a bittersweet irony for Jack Hawk. But now things have turned around completely. "I am full-time with Pre-Paid Legal," he says. "My wife, Camille, a licensed attorney, is quitting her job to stay home with our daughter. I rarely miss my sons' soccer games. In fact, I hardly ever miss their practices. I am their coach!

"I have an office in my home. I don't have employees, leases, payroll, expensive computer networks, loans, or expensive CPAs. In the old business there were only so many hours in the day. If I wanted to expand into another market and generate more money, I would have to hire more people. Today I can get the same leveraged effect without having to hire anyone. I just show the product and the business opportunity and get the same net effect. Instead of putting them into *my* business, I put them into *their* business."

Larry and Mary King (Missouri)

Thanks to good recruiting by Wilburn Smith all the way back in 1983, Larry and Mary King of Walnut Ridge, Arkansas, have been with Pre-Paid Legal for some seventeen years—and they've experienced the roller coaster of our company's ups and downs during that time!

But Larry's belief in what we were trying to do never wavered. "After looking at Pre-Paid I thought it was the best concept I ever saw and I could see how it could help people," he recalls. "I called Mary and told her about Pre-Paid. She remembers me saying it would be easier than shooting ducks with their feet tied on a pond.

"Most of my excitement came from my being a former Arkansas state trooper; I knew firsthand the need for it in our legal system."

Having been an Amway distributor at one time, Larry also understood the power of network marketing. As he puts it, he "saw an explosion coming." It certainly has come for the Kings. "Mary and I are lucky because our whole family is involved with Pre-Paid," Larry says. "Due to the opportunity Pre-Paid Legal gave us, we are now millionaires. We were able to buy several tracts of land, including a four-hundred-acre ranch. We are really able to live the lifestyle most people only dream of.

"The one thing I would say is that to be successful in Pre-Paid, never give up. Don't let anyone steal your dreams because dreams do come true."

Pete and Kim Kowanko (Utah)

Before finding Pre-Paid Legal, Pete Kowanko was an actor "working on his golf swing" and his wife, Kim, was in advertising at Fox Network. Pete says it was "pretty much feast to famine—mostly famine."

233

Then this Los Angeles husband and wife, who now make their home in Heber, Utah, were introduced to Pre-Paid Legal by an acquaintance. Pete recalls: "At first, I thought I'd sell a few memberships and get my lawyers for free. But the more we looked at the product, the more we liked it."

Attending the 1997 National Conference in Oklahoma City convinced the Kowankos to go all out in building their business. "We visited the home office in Ada that same week and decided then and there that we would come to the 1998 convention as executive directors—and we did!" says Pete.

"I like to confess that we probably did almost everything wrong when it came to building our business," he continues. "You name it. Probably the only mistake we didn't make was to quit. The program works if you keep showing up. If you mix a healthy dose of enthusiasm and commitment to the cause of legal access for every American, look out!"

Pete says, "We can grow as big as we dare. We have freedom and we can make a difference in the lives of others. We're creating long-term security for our family. Thank you, God, and thank you, Pre-Paid Legal!"

Ray and Wendy Last (Wisconsin)

Working in the seminar products industry for fifteen years, Ray and Wendy Last of Waukesha, Wisconsin, enjoyed a good income. But they also realized that as soon as they stopped working, everything would grind to a halt.

That's why the Pre-Paid Legal opportunity appealed to them. "In the seminar business," Ray explains, "I would promote the next seminar to pay the speaker and the overhead that goes with an event. With PPL, the product made sense, the company was an open book, and, most important, I took a liking to the leadership right off the bat."

Ray and Wendy say the key to their business success is talking to as many people as they can find. They search for those with an interest and don't waste their time on those who are just not ready.

"This business is great. Too many people have a lottery mentality. We found that if you just do the fundamentals on a daily, weekly basis, the business will really take on a life of its own," Ray says.

"It used to be that a day off meant no income. Strangely enough, our biggest sales week of the year last year was the same week I was out with the flu," states Ray. "I kind of hope that was just a coincidence!

"I no longer dread Monday morning," Ray adds, "and Wendy is able to spend more time with the kids.

"I have seen too many good people try to build their dream with a company that has no real foundation. They put their money, time, and reputation on the line, and one day everything can tumble. I think having a PPL business is like building your dream on a rock."

Larry and Inger Lemke (Washington)

For Larry and Inger Lemke of Bellevue, Washington, their Pre-Paid Legal business is "all or nothing!"

Larry became an associate more than ten years ago. He only stayed active for about three months, but the residual checks kept coming in. "I realized that I had earned thousands in residual income over ten years even though I was completely inactive," Larry says. "The light went on and we became convinced that Pre-Paid Legal is the only genuine residual income opportunity in America today." The Lemkes, who had marketed telecommunications and had owned a franchise, decided to work PPL full-time.

"People with desire tend to be self-starters," the Lemkes explain. "And that is who we've spent most of our time working with." They instruct their new recruits not to get "creative." They say, "Find the most successful people in PPL and quickly learn their key beliefs and strategies and model them. Build this business as if your hair's on fire and take no prisoners!"

Larry is amazed at how fast his business has grown after years of inactivity. "We worked very hard in at least three other network marketing companies, but we've never seen so many successful people so quickly. We believe it is because the timing is so right for the PPL product in our society."

Mike and Nancy Little (Indiana)

Mike and Nancy Little's Pre-Paid Legal success story is another tale of rags to riches. "But it's not just the income we make," says Mike, "It's how we can finally be the people we really want to be."

The Littles are now sending a daughter to one of the best and most expensive colleges in Indiana. "Without Pre-Paid, there would be no way we could afford this," he says. With their PPL income, the Littles also enjoy the luxury of driving nice cars, having a swimming pool, and owing no debt. "We have taken our parents on vacations," they report. "We can donate to our favorite charities. We can do things for our family that we always wanted to do."

Pre-Paid has given Mike and Nancy their time back. For Mike, who previously worked in a meat-packing company and sold insurance, that's a special benefit of owning an independent business. "We're both free from our jobs," he says. "And we enjoy a lifestyle we can't believe."

On Nancy's last day of work at her job, Mike had her picked up at her office in a limo! She had told her boss she was retiring. Confused, the boss said, "You mean, you're quitting. People only retire when they're sixty-five." Nancy replied, "No, you're wrong. You retire when you have enough money to."

The Littles had more than enough!

Rob and Charlene MacKenzie (Ontario)

Rob MacKenzie of Brampton, Ontario, spent twenty-five years as a Toronto police officer. Since his wife, Charlene, was a stay-at-home mom caring for their five children, Rob also worked part-time jobs to earn extra income, including a few in the network marketing industry. "But Pre-Paid legal has been a hundred times better," he reports.

Rob's experience as a police officer convinced him that there would be a big demand for the Pre-Paid Legal product. "Many times I was in and out of homes and businesses and people would ask me for legal advice. When I told them they would have to get a lawyer, they worried that they wouldn't have the money and didn't know who to contact. I developed a passion for the product very quickly!" he explains.

With Charlene working by his side, Rob has earned a "fringe benefit" with Pre-Paid he never had before: "Freedom. We now know what it means. We can do what we want when we want to. It took me twenty-five years on the police force to earn a base salary of $58,000. In our first six months with Pre-Paid we earned over $100,000," he says.

"Without Pre-Paid, I would still be doing shift work and trying to make ends meet every month. Not only have I taken early retirement from the force at age forty-four, which gives me time freedom—we also have financial freedom."

Recruiting is by far the favorite aspect of the business for the MacKenzies. And there's a simple reason for that, according to Rob. "We can really go out and help people and their families. We can make a living while making a difference."

Ryan and Margaret Nelson (Kansas)

Before Pre-Paid Legal, Ryan Nelson traveled worldwide as a combustion engineer. Margaret was in medical sales. Then the Leawood, Kansas, couple's lives changed forever. "I was on my way to Taiwan when someone gave me a tape about Pre-Paid Legal," Ryan remembers. He was about to invest a large amount of capital in a local business when an acquaintance gave him that tape!

Ryan found more than just a great business opportunity. He also found the love of his life, his wife, Margaret. A mutual friend, another Pre-Paid Legal sales associate, introduced the two!

Ryan says he can't emphasize enough that "by listening to other associates who are successful in PPL, this will help you succeed." His most reliable recruiting technique is selling to recruit. "Showing new members how they can possibly earn up to $171.87 on each personal sale is a great recruiting tool." And to close those membership sales, Ryan asks prospects, "How can you afford to be without this coverage? Take care of the people whom you care most about in life and fill out the Will questionnaire."

Ryan sums up, "Pre-Paid Legal has allowed me to get a life. Rather than traveling to work, I just walk into my home office."

Cleve and Dulcie Pickens (Florida, North)

"Sponsoring is the key to my success," says Cleve Pickens of Windermere, Florida. "All you have to do is sponsor three first-level associates. Then help those three get their three. Do that for six levels and you're an executive director. Once you've completed your three executive director legs, you can go as wide as you want. You will have all the money you need to support yourself and your family while you build your empire!

"It really is that easy if you do it."

Cleve was a U.S. Army major and a career military man. After twenty years of service, he began selling insurance and dabbling in different types of marketing. "I've been in a lot of network marketing companies," he says, "but Pre-Paid is the best! I'm making more money with Pre-Paid than from all the others combined. No products to store or deliver, and everyone makes money with Pre-Paid. You can't lose. It's impossible!"

Cleve and his wife, Dulcie, work their business together, earning a six-figure income. They say the marketing plan is easy. "Just sign up new associates every week, help them sign up associates—and repeat!" orders Cleve. "Do as many presentations and make as many contacts a day as you can."

240

Mary and Richard Reed (Minnesota)

Richard and Mary Reed have always been entrepreneurs at heart—but coming from conventional and conservative backgrounds, Richard went the corporate route while Mary tested the waters in different types of business. "We always believed in network marketing, but never had a whole lot of success finding the right company," Mary says.

When Mary started with Pre-Paid Legal, Richard continued on with his successful corporate career. But after twenty-five years at it, he grew tired of that life—tired of making big money for others. He also had become realistically fearful that a younger person could replace him. Mary recalls, "A couple of years ago, when we attended an awards trip for the top producers in Richard's company, we looked around at the cream and didn't see any happiness. What we saw and heard was everyone's dread of going back home and starting on next year's goals. There were bigger goals, split up accounts and territories, more travel, and fewer rewards to look forward to."

The Reeds knew it was now time to venture out on their own. "We've really enjoyed the freedom of working for ourselves and being able to contribute to the launching of PPL in Minnesota," says Mary.

"It's a great feeling to look the doubting relatives in their eyes and proudly tell them that our company has been number one on the American Stock Exchange and on the Forbes list of best small companies in America.

None of the companies any of them have ever worked for has that credibility.

"The awesome part is that it's just beginning!"

Kerry and Patricia Reid (Virginia)

When Kerry Reid was introduced to Pre-Paid Legal by a former employee, he had never heard of the company, but he immediately saw the need for the product—having spent an average of $50,000 each year on legal fees.

Kerry knew he could build a sales force with Pre-Paid because he had done it many times with other companies. "I was looking for a solid company with a product that really performed so that I would only have to build one more time," he says.

Kerry says that his sales technique is to recruit first and introduce his prospects to the business opportunity. "If they aren't interested, then I sell them the membership," he explains.

Kerry and his wife, Patricia, live in Fairfax Station, Virginia, and have two daughters, one of whom is a PPL director. "Heather is my right hand in performing my regional vice president duties."

Mark Riches (Louisiana)

"This is a business—treat it like one." Mark Riches of New Orleans knows the meaning of this phrase, and he keeps a sign hanging in his office to remind him of it.

"You have to treat Pre-Paid Legal like a business," he explains. "You have to learn how to manage your money, organize your time, and manage others. In order to be successful, you have to treat Pre-Paid Legal like your own business and not just a sideline."

Mark advises his new associates to never, never give up. He likes to share the story of the furniture store. "It displayed a sign that said 'Finishers Wanted.' Couldn't that sign apply to this business as well?" he asks. "Finishers wanted. The world is full of starters, but finishers are a rare breed."

For more than ten years, Mark has been president and owner of Harvard Communications, Inc., a telecommunications consulting firm. Because he has always owned his own business, he quickly saw PPL's appeal to so many hardworking Americans who are looking for a better way of life.

Mark credits Pre-Paid Legal with allowing many wonderful vacations with his wife, Jennifer, and their six children. "In the past 12 months," he says, "my family has been to 32 states and 3 countries. PPL gives me the freedom to be with my family."

Mark Riches (Tennessee)

"Before Pre-Paid Legal, I sold long-distance telephone services and made less than $2,000 a month," says Mark Riches. "It was very difficult raising five children on an income like that. We lived in an apartment and struggled every month to make ends meet. My dreams were not being fulfilled. And I was hungry for a real opportunity."

Mark says he found such an opportunity in Pre-Paid Legal. "I joined the Pre-Paid marketing team in 1995 when I was twenty-nine," he reports. "At first, I concentrated mostly on group sales and within two years I was earning $10,000 a month. But our lifestyle didn't change overnight. We had $50,000 in debts to pay off first and we did it in a year!"

In his third year, Mark began to focus on building a sales organization. After some initial struggles, his income doubled again to $20,000 a month! No wonder he calls his story a rags to "Riches" story!

But money wasn't the only reward, according to Mark. "The biggest reward has been the opportunity I've had to spend time with and help raise our children. My wife, Jennifer, and I have seven now, and in 1999 we moved the family from New Orleans to Cookeville, Tennessee. We bought a horse ranch and an eight-bedroom house.

"This year I turn thirty-five," he continues. "It was always my dream to retire at age thirty-five. Although I have the income to do so, I have another problem. When people retire, they begin doing the things they enjoy and there is nothing I do while working for Pre-Paid Legal that I don't enjoy. I love every minute of it. I am changing people's lives. I spend my day helping others get what they deserve and, in return, my income increases.

"I always tell people that ships are safe in the harbor, but that ships were not made for the harbor. My family and I left the harbor and became financially independent through the incredible opportunity of Pre-Paid Legal."

Myrna Riley (Kentucky)

Myrna Riley taught school for sixteen years but had earned no provision for retirement. "My husband was in the corporate world and was frequently transferred, so I never stayed in one school district long enough to earn a pension," she explains. After a transfer to northern Kentucky, Myrna couldn't find a job so she went to work in the insurance securities business.

It was a stroke of luck. She was introduced to Pre-Paid Legal, and although at first she resisted people's efforts to recruit her, "They started showing me their paychecks," Myrna reports. "I knew they were not much sharper than I was. I thought, If they can make this kind of money, I'd better take another look."

"My first sale was in February 1996. I was really glad to finally be in business for myself, without having an inventory, a storefront, or employees. But more important, I could share a program that no one had, everyone needs, and everyone can afford, and also make a really good living doing it."

Myrna says it's more than the good income that makes the business so attractive. "In January 1997 my

245

father became ill and was hospitalized in another state. I was able to take time off to be with my family during a very trying time and my income continued," she relates. "And when helping my mother get things in order after his death, I was able to use my Pre-Paid Legal membership to settle the important issues we had to deal with.

"What more could anyone ask for? I now have a retirement plan, thanks to the renewal income. I own my own profitable business and I'm helping other people make a difference in their own lives. There is a lot to be said for this freedom and independence while I make a nest egg for my children and their families for years to come."

Nick and Gayle Serba (Georgia)

"Use the service." That's the advice of Nick and Gayle Serba of Atlanta. Know what you're selling and you won't be disappointed.

"When you're with a company, it's unusual to feel that the more you get to know it, the more you like it," Gayle explains. "Nick and I are proud to be associated with a company that has integrity, value, and opportunity. Our experience with Pre-Paid Legal has led us to involve friends and family members because we believe so strongly in it."

Before starting their business, Nick managed an insurance agency and Gayle was a Miss Georgia and Miss America runner-up. Three of their four sons are director-level associates and their fourth son soon will be.

The Serbas tell new recruits to always wear PPL's Lady of Justice pin, attend all available meetings and training, and follow the example of those who have really succeeded in the business. When selling memberships, Gayle advises, "Always point out that the cost of not owning it is greater than the cost of owning it."

Mike and Twila Sims
(District of Columbia and Maryland)

Today Mike and Twila Sims are totally sold on Pre-Paid Legal. "It's a fantastic company, offering everyone an opportunity of a lifetime," they say. But this was not always the case.

When Twila signed up as an associate in January 1994, Mike wasn't happy about it. "I had a very negative view of multilevel marketing," he recalls. "Especially since I had given Twila $10,000 to invest in another multilevel program that cost more than we made." But soon Twila's Pre-Paid Legal business took off and Mike began to change his mind.

Then, Twila's mother developed serious health problems and became totally disabled. Caring for her mother took almost all of Twila's time. There was little left to spend on Pre-Paid Legal.

"But despite that fact, an interesting thing happened," Mike reports. "Every month, Twila received a check from Pre-Paid. At first, they were small but then they started to grow to over $1,000."

247

Mike began to wonder what would happen if they both really put their full energies into the business. He worked the business hard, and in four months he was earning more from PPL than from his regular job in corporate America. He resigned to help build the Sims's Pre-Paid Legal business full-time.

"The associate makes an income most people can only dream of," the Simses sum up. "If you persevere, you will achieve your dreams."

Lloyd and Deborah Tosser (Arizona)

For fifteen years before joining Pre-Paid in 1996, Lloyd Tosser poured his heart and soul into the insurance business. He lived to regret it. "I had worked hard to get to what I considered the 'pinnacle' of my insurance career, only to have it yanked away from me," he says. The company he worked for was bought out by a larger firm, drove agents away with the changes, and ended up dissolving Lloyd's division.

But at the time Lloyd and wife, Deborah, also happened to be satisfied Pre-Paid Legal customers. "We used it two times and in both cases it worked great. It's very unusual to find a product that actually works the way it's supposed to and when you need it. We were so impressed, we thought why not sell the product as well?"

Reaching a new and, this time, lasting "pinnacle" of success, the Tossers most appreciate not the money but the way Pre-Paid rewards effort and the changes it has allowed in their lifestyle.

"It seems like a simple opportunity, but it's a rare one," Lloyd says. "The harder you work, the more money you make. Sounds almost silly, doesn't it? But how many companies are left in America where you are rewarded for working hard, where there's no upper limit, and where you don't constantly look over your shoulder, waiting for someone to take it all away from you?" he observes.

"Deb and I work for ourselves now. We're not stuck in morning traffic, white-knuckling the steering wheel while eating an Egg McMuffin. We have a one-minute commute from the bedroom to the office. If we want to work late, we can. If we want to take the day off, we can.

"It's up to us now. We're in control of our own lives."

Sunil and Lori Wadhwa (California)

Before Pre-Paid Legal, Sunil Wadhwa of Foster City, California, was a real estate investor and his wife, Lori, worked for a major airline. Now, they say they're living their dream. Sunil is a full-time associate, while Lori left the airline business to support their PPL business and focus on their two daughters.

Sunil originally passed up on the Pre-Paid Legal opportunity because he had had some unfavorable experiences with multilevel marketing in the past. But he became convinced that the product was one that everyone in America could use.

The Wadhwas, in fact, could have used it themselves in 1990 when they lost more than $800,000 in a business deal. An extremely complex lawsuit required them to spend more than three years of their lives in the court system, fighting five individuals who had defrauded them.

Sunil says, "Unfortunately, it wasn't until 1995 when I was introduced to PPL that I took the time to sit down and see the entire presentation. Lightbulbs, floodlights, and fireworks immediately went off in my head. The experience we had just gone through made it easy for me to realize that we were not alone. Everyone in America needs this service, even the 'lucky' families who don't know it yet."

Sunil tells new associates to "eat, breathe, and sleep PPL; become passionate in what you believe; set forth and do it. Persistency and consistency equal future millionaires!"

Brooks and Celeste Werkheiser (Mississippi)

Brooks Werkheiser is having a good time with his Pre-Paid Legal business. "My energy level and enthusiasm have increased significantly. I have always liked people, but that has also grown."

Before Pre-Paid, Brooks was vice president of a major company and part owner of others. "But for years, my dream has been to run a home-based business with my family. I am beginning to live that dream with Pre-Paid Legal."

With support from his wife, Celeste, and their three children, Brooks reached the executive director position in just eight months. Associates in his organization consider him the master of the soft-sell approach. He describes his favorite recruiting technique as calling or meeting with people and explaining the opportunity, "then allowing them to decide if I can be their sponsor." He firmly believes he's asking people to put their trust in the Pre-Paid opportunity; by signing up, they are allowing him to work with them—not the other way around.

Brooks's bottom line advice for associates trying to build success is simple: "Be trainable, be accessible, and make a long-term commitment."

Mark Wittman (Illinois)

Mark Wittman of Manteno, Illinois, was working for a major electrical utility when a friend saw an ad in the newspaper for Pre-Paid Legal and both of them were introduced to the business.

Mark had enjoyed considerable success at his job. "I started out reading meters and in three years I was bitten by dogs eight times!" he recalls. "I then decided to get as far away as possible from those dogs, so for the next fifteen years I climbed poles and worked on utility wires. I had top seniority, great benefits, and good money—about $70,000 a year!"

But then Mark was "bitten" by the Pre-Paid Legal bug! "In my first month with Pre-Paid, I put sixteen hours into the business and made the same money that I did from working 160 hours at my full-time job. After four months of working the business, my Pre-Paid Legal insomnia (lying in bed with a calculator) became so bad that I just had to quit my job and do the business full-time," he explains.

Mark and his wife, Wendy, achieved the executive director position in just eight months and have been climbing higher ever since. The financial freedom gives them more time to spend with their daughter Cassandra. "I am convinced that Pre-Paid Legal has the greatest work-to-reward ratio," Mark explains. "It has an incredibly generous marketing plan. That, coupled with the unparalleled legal service, the unbelievable need for it, and the timing in today's market, creates an unlimited equal income opportunity for the average person.

"Most people in the United States and Canada are basically drowning in two separate large lakes," Mark continues. "As a Pre-Paid Legal associate I am empowered with two types of life preserver. For those drowning in the legal lake, I can throw them a legal life preserver with a Pre-Paid legal membership. For the millions of people drowning financially, I throw a financial life preserver with the Pre-Paid Legal business opportunity.

"It's very gratifying to be able to positively impact the lives of huge numbers of people!"

252

A Family Affair

For many associates, this business all comes down to freedom. But in saying that, I wouldn't want you to think that our associates are out there alone, left to fend for themselves. We've got a great group of associate leaders at Pre-Paid, and, as I think you can see, they come from all walks of life, every background, and every corner of the country.

But now they have something special in common. They are part of the Pre-Paid Legal family—and it's a family that welcomes new members every day. Remember that time Wilburn was so sick and we worried he wouldn't make it, so we started a prayer chain for him in Branson? Well, each year, right before Christmas we gather up several hundred of our key associates and employees, all their spouses and kids and grandkids, and absolutely invade that place! We go to some concerts, enjoy some great food and socializing, and hear some really interesting speakers, like our friend and Pre-Paid board member Fran Tarkenton.

Fran is, of course, one of our country's great sports legends. But what you may not know is how much he has achieved since retiring from football. He is an astute and gutsy entrepreneur and one of the best motivational speakers I've ever heard. We're very proud that he is now part of our team at Pre-Paid Legal.

Even with all the fun and good cheer at Branson, the highlight for Shirley and me, as well as for many of our

Pre-Paid colleagues, is the Rockettes Christmas Spectacular. At the end of the show, they perform a skit called "The Promise." It's a rendition of the Nativity scene, complete with all the requisite costumes and staging, even live animals. It's one of the most moving things we've ever seen and it brings our Pre-Paid family closer together than any sales meeting ever could. It reminds us all, regardless of our particular faiths, that we are not in this alone. We do it together, and together we are changing lives for the better all across America.

Chapter 9

"OVERNIGHT SUCCESS" AT LAST!

I get a lot of letters. This one in particular caught my eye:

My name is Barbara Pat Brenneman. I received a speeding ticket in August 1998 (41 m.p.h. in a 15-m.p.h. school zone). I faxed the ticket over to Dempsey Roberts & Smith [her Pre-Paid Legal provider firm in Nevada] and they promptly took care of it. They negotiated it to illegal parking with a $150 fine. The fine amount was the same, but this kept four points off my driving record.

I went to sign the agreement at the city attorney's office. It was not what Cindy Sully (my attorney) had agreed to, but instead of calling her office first, I signed it.

When I did call my attorney, she called the city attorney's office but since I had acted before calling them, I had to appear the 28th of September, in court, in person. When the time came, I had not completed anything that was required. I had not attended traffic school or paid anything on the fine.

I was having a serious financial problem and wasn't going to have a place to live in another two days. I walk with a cane and use the bus for transportation. I had moved to Las Vegas and court was in Henderson, which is one and a half hours by bus when you have to transfer.

I called the lawyer's office the morning of the 28th. I was to be in court *that evening* at 6:30 P.M.

I was very upset due to all the other problems I had and now was going to have to tell the judge I had done nothing I was supposed to.

When I talked to Bobbie McFarland . . . at Dempsey Roberts & Smith, she told me there was nothing else she could do. Just to throw myself on the mercy of the court. I started crying and thanked her. I told her I would handle it by myself.

Imagine my surprise when I got to court at 6:30 P.M. in Henderson, Nevada, to find Bobbie waiting for me. She had completely renegotiated the whole deal.

She and Cindy had tried all day to reach the city attorney but could not. Then they spoke to Mr.

Smith, their boss, to ask if it was okay for Bobbie to go to Henderson on her own time to be with me and help make it less difficult for me. Bobbie lives in Las Vegas, too.

I personally think this is above and beyond the call of duty for all involved. If I hadn't already been sold on Pre-Paid Legal, this certainly would do it. . . .

Thank you for offering such a splendid program with law offices that *really* care about their clients.

That's what Pre-Paid Legal is all about to me—helping average people whose problems may seem small to others but to the affected person at the time they're the most important thing in the world.

I hope you're as troubled as I am that justice in America is reserved for all but a privileged few. Somewhere along the way we seem to have accepted the concept that justice is a commodity. If you can't afford it, you can't have access to it. I don't agree!

The rich have access to it. The poor have access to it. The vast majority of people don't and don't know what to do about it.

Lincoln's dream that reverence for the law becomes the political religion of the nation appears to be a hopeless fantasy. Criminals with wealth and connections can find lawyers to twist the truth and the evidence like pretzels and win their undeserved freedom by psychologically profiling and then manipulating jurors. Innocent accused persons without means often find themselves subjected to a law enforcement and media culture that assumes they are guilty until proven innocent. A third of the American people believe that the justice system was in fact designed to be that way.

I don't believe this! I don't agree and I am not willing to accept that concept. I'm driven to change that.

The big corporations can hire batteries of lawyers to beat down even the most justified and modest claims against them made by average citizens. Yet those same corporations can be intimidated out of millions of dollars by predatory trial lawyers peddling frivolous class-action lawsuits in which there are no real victims.

That's what Pre-Paid Legal is all about to me—helping average people whose problems may seem small to others but to the affected person at the time they're the most important thing in the world.

What can we do to reverse these disturbing trends? How can we change the justice system and make it work for Middle America? How can we help the legal profession find its lost compass, and reorient it toward the old ideal of achieving, through the law, a fair and just society for all?

Not by making fancy speeches. All the pleas in the world from the American Bar Association to its member lawyers about doing more pro bono work won't change the fundamental economic realities of the legal business that prevent them from doing so. And we can't wait for the government to reform the legal system. The warrior

lobbyists representing both corporate America and the
trial bar have been waging a battle royal against each
other for years—and they've got lawmakers tied up in
the biggest political traffic jam you've ever seen.

But there is a way America can live up to its promise
of equal justice under law within the present system. We
can do this by embracing a better way to deliver legal services to average Americans and by using the power of the
marketplace to demand for them the very best. To demand for them equal justice under law. Today under the
present system justice is only equal when you can pay for
it. A lawyer recently said to me, "Most Americans need a
lot more justice than they can afford."

At Pre-Paid Legal, our mission is to change that.

After nearly three decades of struggle, we're an
overnight success at last!

o We have more than 800,000 members—individuals and their families who now have unlimited
   access to the best lawyers in the country—and
   the numbers are increasing daily.
o We have more than 200,000 active sales associates—men and women from all walks of life
   who are building independent businesses and se-
   curing their financial future while helping others
   gain access to justice.
o We have a network of provider law firms that
   includes the nation's top lawyers, with a high-
   tech, high-touch system to help them deliver

outstanding customer service and to help us monitor their performance. It has been said that we are fanatics about service. Service had more to do with building McDonald's than the hamburger did. The best customer service is responsible for building Pre-Paid Legal.

o   We have a professional staff of four hundred dedicated, hardworking employees in our Ada headquarters and another hundred off site. These include some of the top experts in the nation in their chosen fields. For example, they just don't make many people like Randy Harp, our chief financial officer and chief operating officer. His skills, competence, and leadership have contributed greatly to Pre-Paid Legal's growth and financial health. Besides all that, he's a workaholic!

And he's not alone. We have great managers, including Jamie Anderson, membership services; Jeanie Anderson, group marketing; Alan Arabi, customer service; Sheila Burris, marketing services; Leslie Fisher, attorney resources; John Long, marketing support; Vicky Mapp, information systems; Greg Patton, human resources; Kathy Pinson, accounting; and Don West, warehouse distribution.

o   We are publicly traded on the New York Stock Exchange, where we have been recognized as the 33rd fastest growing company on that exchange. *Forbes* has named us number 13 on its list of the

200 best small companies in America. This is our fourth consecutive year on that prestigious list.

○ We have no long-term debt, plenty of money in our cash and investment accounts, and a market capitalization of more than half a billion dollars.

○ And we've accomplished all of that as a company without even beginning to tap the true potential of the market. We haven't even hit 2 percent penetration in our home state of Oklahoma. The potential for incredible growth outstripping anything we've yet seen is sitting right before us and we're going to grab it!

Most important of all, our thirty-year "overnight success" as a company means that in the future we can put all our focus where I really want it to be—on opening the doors of justice to millions upon millions of Americans—and Canadians, too! When we don't have to worry quite so much about paying the bills, about being written out of the marketplace by a capricious regulator, or about being denied access to the very best lawyers due to obstacles thrown in our path by the legal

> After nearly three decades of struggle, we're an overnight success at last!

establishment, we have the luxury and the tremendous satisfaction of getting down to the business of helping people with a compelling product. I've said it in almost every chapter so why break my streak now? It's the product more than anything else that defines us as a company and that explains our hard-fought success. We are truly a product-driven company.

It took years of blood, sweat, and tears, but now I can truly say we've perfected our product, won its acceptance, ensured its quality, and married it to the powerful growth engine of network marketing. That's why you're about to witness an explosion of growth at Pre-Paid Legal in the coming decade that will dwarf all that we have achieved over the last three. The best is yet to come. We're primed and positioned for dynamic growth.

But we aren't just sitting around waiting for the future to happen. Not by a long shot. We're busy working on new tools and strategies to help our sales associates build their businesses and push our legal service products out to millions of additional customers.

Pre-Paid Joins the Internet Age

Information technology has been so vital to our ability to improve, customize, and monitor the quality of the legal services our provider law firms offer. Now we are also embracing technology to drive our marketing forward and to improve income opportunities for the associates.

In the fall of 1999 we launched a cyber-based communications platform that will give current and future associates an opportunity to start their own Web-based businesses without the need to develop their own sites. They will be able to enroll customers and recruit other associates through their own personalized Web sites. In addition to developing online leads, they will also have access to e-mail, corporate communications, and an on-line catalog, which includes sales tools, educational materials, and online training.

Anyone who tells you he or she knows exactly where e-commerce is headed in the future—even people who make that their primary business—is not telling you the truth. But we will be riding on top of the wave, ready to take advantage of the opportunities not only to grow our company through online sales, but also to explore the possibility of delivering some legal services and products electronically.

Pre-Paid and the People's Network

One of the greatest challenges facing rapidly growing companies with large, national sales forces—particularly direct-selling and network-marketing companies—is, How do you communicate with those salespeople? How do you make sure they are well trained and fully informed about the latest company and product news? How do you ensure the kind of quality control in sales that we have been able to ensure in product delivery? After all, every one of those sales associates is our ambassador to the public. Not just our growth but our good name is on the line.

Sensing that we had reached a point where this would become a major challenge, Pre-Paid Legal has acquired The People's Network (TPN) and its popular Success Channel, which, via satellite, broadcasts training and motivational programming. Having our own channel to pipe consistent training, information, and company news directly into the homes of our associates will improve their sales skills and money-making opportunities, as well as enhance the image we present to Middle America.

But that's not all that attracted me to TPN. We also gained the services of two outstanding network marketing innovators and organization builders, TPN founders Jeff Olson and Eric Worre. They have already worked wonders in helping our people recruit by developing an easily duplicated system that members can follow to build their own personal organizations. The icing on the cake was some 12,000 network marketers under the TPN umbrella that Jeff and Eric brought with them to boost Pre-Paid's sales force.

Network marketing is facing the same continual stresses and turmoil confronting almost every other industry. We needed leaders who were on the cutting edge of the industry and at the top of their game. TPN brought them to us and is already putting Pre-Paid Legal in the small handful of companies that industry experts say are really doing network marketing the right way.

Oh, Canada!

In a business full of excitement and nail-biting developments over the years, I have to say that our expansion
into Canada, beginning in Ontario and British Columbia provinces in July 1999, comes near the top of the list.
Within six months, we already signed up 10,000 members in Ontario—an initial pace we've rarely seen anywhere else. It has just blasted off! Canada promises to be
a great market for the company, and sales associates now
have a whole new venue in which to recruit other associates and sell products.

I also have to say that some aspects of the entry into
Canada were, in the immortal words of Yogi Berra, "déjà
vu all over again." Once again we are in the position of
introducing a new kind of product in a market that is
unfamiliar with it and winning the acceptance from regulators who have no experience with it.

We were confronted with that old, familiar question:
Are we insurance? If so, we'd have to be regulated like insurance. In Canada, those regulations are extraordinarily
rigid. For example, associates would have to get insurance agent licenses—and you can only get them if you're
going to make insurance your full-time occupation. That
would have blown the most attractive feature of our
business opportunity right out of the water—the ability
to work the business successfully part-time.

But today we've got a lot of experience in working
constructively with regulators and we did just that in

Canada, structuring the products to meet their concerns. Now it's steady as she *grows!*

With Pre-Paid Legal an international business (I like the sound of that!), what about introducing our products in other countries, particularly those with legal systems somewhat similar to our own, from Australia to Japan to Europe?

I must get a couple of calls a week from very smart and experienced people saying we should do that. After all, the international arena now accounts for most of the growth in U.S. network marketing companies and in many cases for the lion's share of their sales and recruiting.

I won't rule it out. In fact, it would be kind of rewarding to open the doors of justice and entrepreneurship in other societies as we have done here. But here's the difference between our company and others. Most network-marketing and direct-selling companies sell consumer products that are already being used regularly by most Americans. The only suspense is: From whom will they buy them and at what price?

Our legal service products are entirely different and very unique. Virtually all Americans have purchased a household product, bought vitamins or food supplements, or made long-distance phone calls. But most have never had a pre-paid legal plan. With less than a 1-percent market penetration in the United States, we've got a lot of work to do right here at home. And with our track record of successful sales so high whenever we get the chance to tell someone about our products, why not focus first on all this "low-hanging fruit"?

Back to the Future

It's been thirty-one years since the car accident that changed my life. From that adversity, a simple idea was born and from it a simple question was asked: Why should any American be denied access to equal justice? Why should justice be the private preserve of the rich and powerful? I'm so grateful that I was given an opportunity to ask that question, provide an answer, and help make our country a better place. When I think back on the years when we struggled to do that, it's hard not to remember those who made the journey with us—and those who did not.

I find myself thinking about the greatest man I have ever known, my father, Allen Stonecipher, who passed away in 1977. He would have been so proud of his son and what I, with the help of so many, have been able to put back into the community where we both grew up. The company we built would amaze him and my mother, who passed on in 1984. I think it might even have made up for the fact that they could no longer tell people their son was a schoolteacher!

Shirley's dad left us back in 1963, years before we even began this incredible journey. If he could only see how all over the country, sales associates and their spouses rush up to Shirley after the speech-making is done to ask for some advice, make a suggestion, and just thank her for being part of what is really their company. She gives Pre-Paid Legal so much of its heart and soul and everyone knows it and appreciates it. I know how hard it is for her now to play such an important role in everything we do and still visit her ninety-year-old mother every day in the nursing home. Some days Shirley is not really sure if her Mom even recognizes her, and those days are really tough.

I find myself also thinking about Charlie Walls, who left his beloved Laverne alone in 1998. It was Charlie who helped me break my folks' hearts, though they'd never admit it, by coaxing me away from teaching and into business. It was Charlie who pushed a scared young man out onto the center stage of sales all by himself. He followed all the developments at Pre-Paid with great interest and pride and would have loved to have seen the many chapters of history we have yet to write.

Nick Pope was the founder of National Foundation Life, the company I went to work for when I left teaching. He became one of my mentors and biggest supporters. I wish he could see us now!

What a loss to lose Nick and Charlie. How I wish I could still call them and ask for advice. I have gained so much from their coaching, training, advice, and encouragement. I did the eulogies at both of their funerals and considered it such an honor to be asked by their families.

These two men changed Shirley's life and mine, and because of them, we have been able to change the lives of others. Thanks, Charlie and Nick!

Somewhere up there Rick Haney is smiling down on all of us, telling us, in spirit at least, never to give up, never to let the obstacles and reversals get the better of us. On a table in my office I keep Rick's old battered salesman's briefcase just as he left it, contents and all. It was—and is—a briefcase full of hope and inextinguishable optimism. I look at it on a regular basis. As long as his briefcase is there, he is still with me. How I miss him, I can't tell. His sons and grandkids come to see me. I want them to know what I knew about Rick Haney.

And there's Jim Hite, a Pre-Paid Legal Services board member from Atlanta, Georgia—too soon gone, but whose wise counsel will never be forgotten.

Yes, I think a lot about all the people who made this journey with Shirley and me, who travel with us in person or in spirit. But mostly, I'm thinking about the future. The future of our sons and grandchildren and the many young people I meet when I'm invited to speak at their high school and college commencements.

They often ask me what are the keys to success in life. And my answer may not be particularly eloquent but, judging by the nods of their heads, I think it is a sound answer that makes a lot of sense.

First, you have to really be sold on what you are doing or selling. Your biggest sale in life is always to yourself. Really believing in what you're doing will not only give you a competitive edge, it will make you a happier and more fulfilled person. You can't see that which you don't believe. It helps if you believe your product or service can change people's lives.

Second, you have to have a quality that Thomas Edison called "sticktoitiveness." You can't quit even if you look like an idiot out there all by yourself. You just have to keep on going no matter what others are saying, no matter how many roadblocks are thrown in your way, no matter how much work is required or how tired you are. Sticktoitiveness—it's such an important and all too rare quality that old Tom Edison had to invent his own word for it! I sometimes wonder where I got the tremendous amount I needed to survive and get where we are today.

Third and finally, make sure that what you do helps other people. The older I get, the more I find myself focusing on the larger purpose that drives what I'm doing. Helping others, embracing a cause larger than yourself—they're easy words to say, much tougher words to really mean. Ask yourself, Do you really want to help others or just yourself? Zig Ziglar said, "You can get anything you want in life if you're willing to help others enough." I believe it!

So many times over the last thirty years I have been so caught up with the day-to-day challenges of keeping Pre-Paid Legal afloat and alive that I found myself losing sight of what building this company was all about. That's why I say that reaching the position of strength we're in today—where practically our singular focus can now be on the fundamentals of getting our product and our business opportunity out to as many people as possible—has been a great place to reach. Today, a letter from a woman like Barbara Pat Brenneman saying that we helped her in a time of great need means so much more to me than the latest pronouncement from some Wall Street pundit on whether our stock will or should go up or down. Our stock will do just fine, thank you, as long as we keep the focus on helping more people like Barbara. Service is what and *all* we sell!

We've only written the opening chapters of the Pre-Paid Legal Story. They're just the warm-up act. I'm filled with plans and dreams and great hopes for the future. Every day we're pushing this wonderful country a little bit closer to the time when equal justice under law will be a promise fulfilled.

It hasn't been easy—and it won't be. But every time I find

> You can't quit even if you look like an idiot out there all by yourself. You just have to keep on going no matter what others are saying, no matter how many roadblocks are thrown in your way, no matter how much work is required or how tired you are.

myself getting a little down, sinking low in my chair as the day's problems pile up, I lift up my eyes and gaze over at the wall where, staring right back at me, is a framed quotation from Theodore Roosevelt. Rick Haney had given it to me years ago:

Dare greatly. It is not the critic who counts, not the man who points out how the strong man stumbled or where the doer of deeds could have done better. The credit belongs to the man who is actually in the arena, whose face is marred by dust and sweat and blood, who strives valiantly, who errs and comes short again and again, who knows the great enthusiasms, the great devotions and spends himself in a worthy cause. Who at the best knows in the end the triumph of high achievement, and who at the worst if he fails at least fails while daring greatly so that his place shall never be with those cold and timid souls who know neither victory nor defeat.

Index

A

African Americans, racial profiling of, 18–20, 34–35

America
justice in, 3–4. *See also* Justice system
litigious culture of, 57. *See also* Lawsuits
opportunity for success in, 97–98

American Bar Association
as embracing pre-paid legal coverage, 136, 142
estimates of percent of world's lawyers in America by, 54
open panel approach required by, 142
pleas for more pro bono work by, 258
public opinion survey of respect for lawyers by, 55
response to lack of accessibility to justice system of, 54
statistics about legal situations by, 23
survey of American justice by, 39–41

American Stock Exchange, Pre-Paid Legal Services on
listing of, 143
as number one company, 241

Amway, Federal Trade Commission ruling on, 135–136

Antitrust laws, paying "regular and customary" legal fees found in violation of, 137

Attorney fees, excessive billing of, 140–141

Attorney general of Oklahoma, positive view of Pre-Paid Legal Services of, 142–143

Attorney referrals, 138–139
quality control in, 139–140, 142

Attorneys. *See also* Legal establishment
attitude of, 92
for class action suits, 49–50, 58
corporate, 28
costs of, 22, 90–91
customer service by, 81–83, 90, 91, 140, 260
disillusionment of, 55–56
need for, 23–25
number of American, 3
over-billing by, 140
pro bono work of, 54, 88
profit from tort system of, 47–48
response to participating in pre-paid legal plan by, 139

Attorneys for Pre-Paid Legal Services
access to top, 8–9, 61, 67–68, 71–72, 74–76, 81–85
constant evaluation of, 90
document review by, 72, 78, 79
high-tech quality monitoring of, 85–87
IRS audit services by, 74, 78
network of, 259–260
phone calls and letters from, 72, 78, 79
preferred member discount by, 71, 74–75, 78
traffic accident and damage recovery by, 73–74
traffic defense by, 73, 78
trial defense by, 74, 78, 80
will preparation by, 72–73, 78, 239

Auto clubs
Pre-Paid Legal Services marketed as, 131–136